Nick Ward was born in Geelong, Australia, in 1962. He began writing and directing for the theatre while studying at Cambridge University, winning three Scotsman Fringe First awards in 1983–4. He studied at film school in Bristol and went on to write and direct *Eastwood* (1985). After working as Christopher Nupan's assistant on a series of classical music documentaries, he had an association with the National Theatre's studio, culminating in *Apart from George* (1987) and *The Strangeness of Others* (1988), for both of which he received the 1988 George Davine Award. *Dakota Road* is his first film as writer/director.

Director Nick Ward with actress Charlotte Chatton (Jen).

Dakota Road

NICK WARD

faber and faber

LONDON · BOSTON

First published in 1991
by Faber and Faber Limited
3 Queen Square London WC1N 3AU

Photoset by Parker Typesetting Service Leicester
Printed in England by Clays Ltd St Ives plc
All rights reserved

Nick Ward is hereby identified as author of
this work in accordance with Section 77
of the Copyright, Designs and Patents Act 1988

A CIP record for this book is available from the British Library

ISBN 0-571-16302-5

For Rachel

Contents

Dakota Road was first shown at the 1991 Berlin Film Festival.
The cast included:

BERNARD CROSS	Matthew Scurfield
JEN CROSS	Charlotte Chatton
RAIF BENSON	Jason Carter
ALAN BRANDON	Alan Howard
MAN IN TRAIN	David Bamber
JOAN BENSON	Liz Smith
DOUGLAS STONEA	David Warrilow
AMY CROSS	Rachel Scott
MAUD CROSS	Amelda Brown
AMERICAN PILOT	Alexis Denisof
Director of Photography	Ian Wilson
Editor	William Diver
Production Designer	Careen Hertzog
Sound Recordist	Simon Okin
Music	Paul Stacey
Executive Producer	Sarah Radclyffe
Producer	Donna Grey
Director	Nick Ward

A Working Title Film.
Stills by Olly Hoeben.

Notes on the Making of *Dakota Road*

(Interview conducted by Rachel Inman, October 1990)

BACKGROUND

Why did you decide upon the interview form to make these notes about your work?
Perhaps it's to do with the training I've given myself as a playwright to try to explore all sides of an argument, which means that however passionately and firmly I might believe something, or reach some conclusion, I have an irresistible urge to contradict myself. As a result I find it difficult to write or even think in other than dialogue form. More simply put, and this is not something I'm particularly proud of, I'm insecure about expressing myself in prose, although I find it relatively easy to express my ideas in conversation.

Do you keep a notebook?
Yes, and I'm very particular about it. It has to have a black hard cover and contain squared paper, so that I can make notes both vertically and horizontally – I suppose a kind of graphic representation of my self-contradictions. For the most part, the result is a mixture of extreme order, in almost illegibly small writing, and huge disorganized scrawls about ideas for scripts or characters. I know that I'm ready to write a new script when I look back over my notebooks and discover that ideas that I thought related to four or five different stories have somehow combined and seem containable within a single script. I used to lose a lot of energy trying to force this process, but I'm learning to trust that the ideas will come together eventually, and the one thing I must do is write things down as they occur, however absurd they may seem at the time.

Is there an image which comes to mind as the starting-point of the film?
I find it difficult to pinpoint the starting-point because I lived in the Fens for part of my childhood, so I was living through, experiencing, its landscape and its people. Perhaps the fact that I

arrived there as an eight year old from Australia might explain why, looking back, I always seemed to be looking at things from a certain distance. But maybe I'm just projecting an objectivity which at the time I'm sure I lacked. I do, however, remember those first impressions of this dead flat, waterlogged landscape beneath the shadow of Ely Cathedral, which was visible for miles in all directions. I think I was probably fascinated by what made the Fens different, unique. I remember, very clearly, my mother telling me that we were going to live in a place called the Isle of Ely, but that it wasn't an island any more. I found this fascinating – and still do.

Why?
It's the man-madeness of it. It's an unnatural landscape, yet one which feels relentless, empty, open – but is also a landscape which contains its history as a wild marshland and is full of secrets. The black peat soil is often throwing up prehistoric bog oaks, a perpetual reminder of what this place used to be like before it was drained. A natural hideout, through the ages, for outlaws and criminals. In fact, the Fen people still have within them a sense of their own difference, a kind of independence, which is rarely articulated and often manifests itself as an unfriendliness to strangers. It's a kind of stubborness. But once those barriers have been dropped, there is a warmth and loyalty and a dead-pan, slightly surreal, sense of humour.

So the round-about answer to your question is that the starting point was the people and the landscape and the interrelatedness of the two.

As for more specific images which are echoed in the film, there are two which come to mind. One is of two sisters walking through the Fen, one a few steps ahead of the other, as if they are tied together by an invisible thread. The other is of the outstretched body of a man in a church. Somehow the two images were linked, and they are both in the finished film. At the time I didn't know what they were leading to. They were the first imaginings. In fact the second, the man lying down in the church, was given expression in a play I wrote in 1987 called *Apart from George*. But the image was originally a cinematic one, although at the time I had no foreseeable opportunity of making a film (which was just as well, because I don't think I would have been ready) and it was as a result of seeing *Apart from George* that Working Title offered me a commission to write and direct a film for them.

Are there links between your theatre and film work?
Theatre and film can almost be defined as each others' opposites – they work in very different ways. The theatre director has much less control over the audience's relationship to the story. In the theatre you can only really 'pull focus' in wide shot, and each member of the audience gets a different point of view of the action. The theatre director also has to be prepared to hand the production over to the actors, because, in good theatre, the production should really belong to them. Although a 'cinematic' form of theatre can be very effective, film-making which is derived from the theatre rarely seems to work. It's one of the problems afflicting British cinema, because it's a culture which is rooted in theatre and literature.

I found *sex, lies and videotape* very interesting in this respect, because on the surface it didn't seem to be using the language of cinema to its best advantage – and yet it was resolutely a film. I think this is because Soderberg was using, for him, the best means of telling a wonderfully written, complex story, which was obviously very personal to him. The reason he was able to do this so effectively is partly because he is very talented and partly because he comes out of a film-making tradition where the dangers of 'theatricality' – a group of characters in different configurations talking in rooms – was never obvious to him. It's one of the best films I've seen recently.

I suppose what I'm saying is that there are rules – the less theatre in film-making the better – but the rules are there to be broken. As far as *Dakota Road* is concerned, despite the fact that the theatre work I was doing after leaving film school was in some ways a substitute or rehearsal for film-making, I was almost overly anxious because the film had some of its thematic origins in *Apart from George*. I hope I was successful in this respect; *Dakota Road* took two years to write, through five drafts, whereas *Apart from George* took five days – it was an outburst.

The area of my work where there is probably the most overlap between theatre and film is in working with actors – with the rider that there is a big difference between stage and screen acting. For instance Rachel Scott, whose performance as Amy is one of the things I'm most pleased with in *Dakota Road*, simply couldn't have played the part on stage, because she has absolutely no technical training. The reverse is also true – actors who have a brilliant stage presence and facility can often come over very theatrically on film. There really is such a thing as screen presence – and a movie camera is the best lie-detector ever invented. However, the fundamental ways I have of enabling an actor to truthfully inhabit a role are very similar.

You said you enjoyed sex, lies and videotape – *what other recent films have you enjoyed?*
I liked Kieślowski's *Decalogue*, particularly *A Short Film about Killing*. He can render the most complex emotions with the most seemingly simple means. He is only interested in telling stories with a purpose, but never gets preachy or prescriptive. But the film I enjoyed most was Edgar Reitz's *Heimat*. I saw it twice in the cinema and I'd like to watch all of it again. It had an epic, generative, sweep – always teetering on the brink of soap opera while at the same time tackling some of the most important, world-changing events, thoughts and innovations of this century – and all told through brilliantly realized characters.

I tend to enjoy films most when I've never seen any of the actors before. I love to feel that a film has discovered its actors: it makes it easier to care about and get involved with the characters. When I'm watching a big star, it can make the character less interesting. There are exceptions to this, of course. The great actors are the ones who pull a crowd, but always surprise them.

Whether they are stars or not, that's the only kind of actor I'm interested in, both as a director and as a member of the audience.

There are exceptions to this, as well – a vital ingredient in Hitcock's calculations was the wedge than can be driven between the predictability of a star's performance and the tricks that can be played on the character by the plot. That was his unique gift. This is not true of all his films, but often he would set an actor off on a seemingly preordained, sometimes rather wooden performance, and make the character interesting by inflicting certain events upon them. He tends to be less successful when he attempts a thought-out, psychological explanation for his characters' behaviour. Hitchcock himself is really the most interesting character in his films. At his most disturbing and effective he is a sadist inflicting his will upon submissive characters to satisfy an audience, and the characters he most enjoyed inflicting his sadism on were the women.

Who are your main influences?
I have been influenced as much by certain people as by film-makers or writers. There have been some people in my life who have really helped me by giving me a sense of purpose and confidence. As for films, I have extremely eclectic taste, so it is difficult to name names, but the films I like best are the ones that don't remind me of other films. I like films which are telling their own story and not trying to be something else.

Influence is actually a very difficult thing to admit to. Partly because I feel I have outgrown certain influences which seemed very important a few years ago. So it is easy to try and deny and disown influences, because I feel I have moved on. The further back in my memory I go, the more I might try to deny the importance of certain things.

Specifically to *Dakota Road*, I must say that the films of Ingmar Bergman, particularly *Winter Light*, exerted a traceable influence. When I first saw his films I was particularly struck by the intensity of the performances and the unity which existed between camera, director and actor. Also, at that time, I was very taken with the themes of his films, because I felt they somehow echoed my own experiences as a child in Ely, which has a very particular religious atmosphere. Although I found it oppressive in its authority and orthodoxy, it was also a place in which my imagination could run free.

But, apart from television, which was not a particularly important feature of my childhood, I didn't discover the intoxication of cinema until quite late on. The only cinema in Ely, the Rex, closed down through lack of interest when I was about ten – so it was never really available to me. But special trips to the cinema are among the most memorable events of my childhood.

Can you say more about the writing process?
Not as easily as I can talk about other aspects of my work. All I can really do is describe the technical, organizational aspects of it. This always seems like *most* of the work, but of course the discipline and the actual writing down is only the tip of an iceberg, which, if I were to describe, would probably make very little sense. What I'm talking about is the kind of *state* I'm in when I write, or when I'm getting down to write. This is often preceeded by hours or days of preparing myself, psyching myself up, to write – a tortuous process, taking the form of a mental checklist. Where does the scene fit into the structure? What exactly do the characters really want, beneath the surface of the dialogue? Is what they want too obvious? Or is it so unclear that the scene shouldn't be there at all?

Then I may mentally act out some aspects of a particular character's need. Literally, as I'm walking down the street, I'm getting the character under my skin – looking at the world through the character's eyes – asking myself questions: 'Why am I so lonely?'; 'What makes me happy?'; 'What is my sexuality?'; 'How do I love?' Of course, most of the characters couldn't begin to answer these questions, but not until I know which questions they *can't* answer can I begin to write the scene for them. Also, often reluctantly, I recognize that all the characters represent some, more or less hidden, aspect of myself. It's as if they are shards of my own personality, which although I might only inadequately understand, I convert by a strange process into the emergent personalities of the characters. So there's a constant battle between the formal, scene-building elements and the much more interesting, darker currents which make me a writer in the first place. A kind of fear, incomprehension: a state of being in a trance or a dream. Only when these stages have been gone through – and they may take two minutes or a month – can I write.

All this has a direct link to the work the actors will do and to my other work, as a director, because I tend to have explored the possibility of the characters in performance. I have mentally improvised. The odd thing is that, very often, having prepared a scene like this, I'll sit down to write it and quite unexpectedly write a completely different scene, involving characters I wasn't thinking of. Often it's these scenes, written without any conscious preparation, which remain unchanged. Although the scene bears no overt relation to the one I was planning, often the one I was planning is no longer necessary. The problem, the unwritten scene, has solved itself by being written elsewhere. Usually the actual writing of a particular scene takes no time at all. I write it very quickly, initially in a kind of shorthand, omitting the characters' names and any form of punctuation. It's a bubble of high energy, which bursts when I have finished the scene.

You speak of complex emotions – what do you mean by this?
Quite simply that I think cinema works best when it reaches its audience on more than one level. Too often I hear dialogue in a film and I'm thinking, these characters must be meaning more than what they are saying, and what they're saying can't be all that the scene is about, but too often it's all there is. The film is not demanding a complex response, the picture telling us one thing, the sound and music another, and beneath the surface of the dialogue, the characters misleading themselves and each other – saying one thing and meaning another.

In this respect I was very fortunate to be making *Dakota Road* for Working Title, but I think there are certain aspects of the film business which actively discourage such an approach. The most obvious are the producers who have ceased to view films for themselves. They are forever closing themselves off from a film's possibilities because they double-guess a commercial response from a potential audience, and once they've taken that step they stop taking risks and dictate both the content and execution of the film to meet this predicted response. But I believe passionately that audiences love complexity; they want to be drawn in, to make choices about whether a character is in the right or wrong – in other words to get thoroughly twisted up in a film. For this reason I think risk-taking is an essential part of commercial film-making.

For my taste, the only films which are memorable are the ones which allow a layered engagement. I'm not talking about deliberately confusing an audience with elliptical dialogue, lack of narrative or wilful obscurity – quite the reverse, the films I like best are the ones with the strongest narratives – but, more importantly, with the most interesting characters. Certainly the key to all my work as both writer and director is character-based. You can have the most spectacular location and camera set-up in the world, but if the characters' predicament isn't of interest, it won't work – well not for me, anyway.

Do you think Dakota Road *works in this way?*
I hope so. It's not really for me to say. I certainly intended the characters to be interesting. I remember when I was coming round to writing the first draft of the script, I spent most of the summer of 1988 riding a bike around East Anglia and the Fen country, slowly letting things work themselves out: checking out the landscape, revisiting partly-remembered childhood haunts, but again and again the central demand I was making of myself was that each of the characters must have a story to tell.

Although I knew early on that on one level the central narrative was the Jen and Raif love story, I also knew that the film would only be what I wanted it to be if all the characters were in some way or other changed by the course of events – the story – and that they should all, whether consciously or not, touch each others' lives. So it would be a web of relationships – separate lives touching others.

What surprised me in the editing of the film was that after the first assembly, which ran at 131 minutes, I temporarily lost confidence in holding on to all of the stories, and tried to cut some of the narrative lines back. I was hoping that the result would have more narrative drive, but I found that the film lost out, that if any of the characters were deprived of a relationship, things began to fall apart. So, although the final running time is only about 90 minutes, most of the stories remain in the same relation to the whole as they did in the shooting script.

I hope that the film will work in different ways for different people. As we got closer to the final cut and finishing the picture, this started to be true, even for the small group of producers, financiers and people who had been closely involved in the production, who saw its progress through the editing. They began to disagree about their attitude to particular scenes and characters. When that started to happen I knew that the film was beginning to work in the way that I intended.

FINANCE AND PRE-PRODUCTION

How was the film financed?
The script was developed at Working Title. Having written the third draft there was quite a long pause until I heard whether it was going to attract the necessary finance. I now know that it was much more touch and go than I thought at the time. Although the silence which met this draft – which I knew to be an accurate reflection of the various script conferences I'd had with Alison Jackson and Sarah Radclyffe – was painful, I'm sure it would have been much more dispiriting to know exactly how hard it was for Working Title to raise the money. I was very well protected from this process.

I think the initial budget came out at about £1.6–£1.7 million. The problem was that this figure was too large to be financed solely by a combination of Channel Four and British Screen, which is the usual route for a small-budget film undertaken by Working Title.

How was the problem resolved?
A new scheme called the British Film Partnership which had been developed over a number of years by Simon Relph of British Screen and a group of independent producers, all of whom had become frustrated by the increasing difficulty of funding interesting low-budget films in this country. The scheme had got to the stage where they needed a script which could act as a trial film. *Dakota Road* landed on Simon's desk at the right time. So after a certain amount of discussion we took the plunge.

What were the implications of the British Film Partnership?
On purely financial terms, it meant that we could make the film

for just over £1 million, so it provided a very substantial saving. However, there were tremendous difficulties to overcome because it represented such a new approach. Again, I was very protected in this because of the work of Donna Grey, the producer.

The broad outline of the scheme was as follows. All members of the crew and cast were participants in the film's revenue – as opposed to profit – in foreign sales, and in return they would all work for a basic salary. The number of percentage points of the revenue they would be entitled to would be calculated in proportion to their overall earnings for the duration of the film. Overtime provision, which is usually a large slice of the production budget, would be avoided in favour of a strict forty-hour week. This had important implications regarding the exact planning, with Donna, of a shooting schedule which I could be sure of adhering to. Under the Film Partnership there was also a much less rigid adherence to the traditional demarcations in the operation and crewing of the film.

None of these things struck me as being particularly strange. *Dakota Road* was my first full-length film, so I had nothing to compare it to. Besides, the scheme seemed entirely to do with film-making. However, inevitably, there was a lot of work to be done, primarily by Donna Grey and the originators of the Film Partnership, with the various unions. These negotiations almost reached a stalemate on several occasions. I was busy casting and preparing for the shoot, so Donna protected me from the potential bad news. The unions' eventual attitude was to let the film go ahead – some were more reluctant than others – and to assess the consequences at the end.

What was the result?
The implications are still being weighed up by both the unions and the Film Partnership Committee. The result for me and the crew was a very good atmosphere on the set. We tended to work short Fridays and Mondays, which gave the crew a long weekend off after each week's shooting – thereby keeping everybody well rested and the morale high. There was also a real feeling of commitment to the film. People who didn't like the sound of the Film Partnership didn't take part. So there was a natural filtering

xviii

system and we ended up with a crew who had all made the decision to make this particular film. I was amazed at how many members of the crew told me that they had never been happier on a film – not least because they weren't working the usual exhausting number of hours.

The fact that the smooth running of the scheme was dependent on my keeping to schedule was a responsibility I took very seriously. Given the amount of goodwill people were entrusting to me, I knew that I must keep to my side of the bargain. If we worked forty-three hours one week, I'd aim to work thirty-seven the next. I think, in the end, it did average out to forty hours a week. In this respect I must give credit to Willie (A.J.) Wands, the First Assistant Director, who was a tireless motivator on the set, and a great personal support to me.

Did the fact that most of the finance was provided by a television company affect the way that you made the film?
Although *Dakota Road* was only possible because of Channel Four's backing, I never once *saw* it as television. However, I do think it's a problem for the identity of British film-making.

The fact that Channel Four has been responsible for a kind of renaissance in small-scale film-making is without doubt. But one of the results is that the relationship between television money and cinema has left film-makers slightly confused and divided in their intentions. For instance, both Ian Wilson, the cameraman, and I wanted to shoot *Dakota Road* in cinemascope – it's without doubt a 'scope landscape – but this was as out of the question as the idea of shooting in black and white. The reason: without panning and scanning, it's an unacceptable format for the television audience. Furthermore, avoiding television-framing (centre-framing) both at the shooting stage and at the transmission stage, by use of 'letter-boxing' – strips of black above and below the frame to compensate for the difference between the shape of a 35mm print and the shape of a television screen – is considered a major concession.

Britain is actually very good at television drama, and there is always a badly articulated debate about whether there really is any difference between cinema and television. I firmly believe they are completely different. So beyond being a culture based in literature and theatre – our film industry is often bound to television in both attitude and finance.

What happened in pre-production?

We went into official pre-production in early January 1990, which was when Donna Grey came on to the film. My overriding feeling, looking back, was that I didn't really believe it was going to happen. I'd wanted it for too long. One part of me has remained in disbelief ever since. Another part of me, a larger part, was saying, 'It's one thing to make a film, but I want it to be a good film.'

When I got the 'green light' I rejoiced for about ten minutes, then I got down to work on preparing the shooting script, casting and crewing, working with Donna on the schedule, and spending any time I could on location recces. Certainly in term of the number of hours worked and the number of decisions to be made, pre-production was in many ways much more demanding than the actual shooting of the film.

Why?

For the simple reason that I didn't sleep at night until I'd found the right solution to any given problem, and there was a seemingly endless list of unresolved problems – and the awareness that any wrong decision at the pre-production stage could potentially have a damaging knock-on effect later.

Was casting difficult?

I enjoyed the casting process and I was very fortunate to be working with Sarah Bird, who was the casting director. She was very sympathetic to the film and tireless in wanting to get the casting right. I think the fact that she had just moved from years of working at the BBC, and was relishing the spirit of independence which reigns in Michelle Guish's office, was another reason she seemed to enjoy working on *Dakota Road*.

Casting was a very important time for me because for the first time I had to be very clear about the characters, who until then had existed only in my imagination. Often a character only becomes clear through the casting process, with different actors bringing out different aspects.

How do you approach auditions?
I don't really enjoy auditions – there's never enough time to get to know people, and the actors are usually very nervous. It's often the actors who don't read well off the page, or who appear most nervous at the first meeting, who will turn out to be the best choice. The director has to be able to read between the lines of an audition and to see into the future – to look at a potential performance – while at the same time keeping the atmosphere relaxed, assessing how the actor might come over on screen, and how they will fit into the overall balance of the casting, taking into account the mix of personalities, quite apart from deciding whether it's going to be a good creative partnership. So a lot is going on in what might only be a ten-minute audition, which is why recalls are so important, and also why I try to avoid seeing too many actors in one day.

If you're meeting famous actors, the pressures are very different. Because it is assumed you'll know their work, auditioning in the usual sense is out of the question: usually you're lucky if you get a meeting prior to offering a part. I have always resisted offering an actor a part without first meeting them – it seems to me to be a recipe for disaster.

Was there pressure to cast famous names?
Not really. I did talk this through with Sarah Radclyffe and she completely agreed that 'famous faces' could destroy the heart of *Dakota Road* – unless they were absolutely right for the parts, of course. So we decided that it was in parts like Joan, Alan and Douglas that we could cast well-known actors, but for the rest it shouldn't be a governing condition.

I think the whole question of casting famous names in British films is a bit of a blind alley. I think that big names in the theatre and well-known faces on television rarely make a significant, quantifiable impact in the cinema. I think that too often the best actors for the role are passed over because the producers or financiers haven't heard of them, and they've usually only heard of them if they've seen them on television – so it's a vicious circle. In America or on the continent British theatre and television 'marquee' names mean very little. I was very lucky not to be burdened with these kinds of pressures, which is certainly one of the freedoms of working on a small budget.

When you were looking for locations, did you have particular places in mind?
What made the process of location-hunting so hard was that I'd written the script from my memory of actual places and buildings – but in the process of transforming them into fiction, I'd either changed them beyond recognition, or if the original models did feel right, they weren't available to us.

Looking for locations was the most physically exhausting part of pre-production – driving for hours along every Fenland road on the map, and many which weren't. It was the only time that I missed radio and theatre directing, where a sense of place is created almost entirely in the audience's imagination. I can't go back to the Fens now without seeing houses which we 'auditioned' for Alan Brandon's house or churches which 'showed potential'. It's a bit sad – it's almost as if *Dakota Road* has temporarily hijacked my relationship with the landscape.

PRODUCTION

What about rehearsals?
The rehearsals were important for several reasons. They gave the writer in me a chance to hand over to the director. I cut down and rewrote some of the dialogue when I heard how it was coming off the page. The rehearsals also gave the actors a chance to get to know the characters and each other.

Did the actors suggest many changes?
It's usually obvious when something isn't working, but I have a rehearsal ground-rule which is that the writer will rewrite the scene later on. This ensures that I don't get into a free-for-all in the rehearsal room. I then bring in the amended scene later and we find out whether it's working.

Do you make room for improvisation?
I regard all rehearsing as a form of improvisation, although these days I rarely use improvisational techniques. Now, I'll more often use storytelling techniques – simple ways of locating the actor in the emotion of the scene or character.

Do you enjoy working with actors?
Going into *Dakota Road*, working with actors was the area I felt most confident about. I very rarely feel inhibited or awkward with actors – and I never forget how difficult what they do is. Above all, I try to give them the space they need to act in – both in the writing and in the directing.

How did the mood of the rehearsals transfer to the set?
One of the most important things for me is to try to never let the actor feel the pressure. If they're doing what they can do best, the internal pressure, the concentration on the scene, the interaction, will leave them absolutely no room for anything else. So even if the light is failing, I won't hurry the actor. Often when a scene wasn't working, I'd have a word with Willie Wands and he'd usher the entire crew off the set to take the pressure off, and we'd slowly rebuild the scene together.

It's also important not to let the actors hurry each other. I have to engineer ways of making them accommodate each other. An actor's selfishness is natural and often entirely unselfconscious. I'd never say, 'you're being very selfish here' – rather, I'd try and open up the possibilities of a shared playing of the scene. Invariably, it will suddenly start to feel real to them as well. A door opens and things begin to flow.

If things continue not to flow, I have a mental checklist of possible reasons. Is the script right? Would changing a word or phrase help? Is an actor blocking something which they don't want to expose? What do I have to do to get these actors to trust each other?

I only get impatient if I feel that an actor is bringing some personal baggage into the scene, which is getting in the way: if all their concentration isn't on finding the truthful moment, if they are willing to settle for second best or if they are refusing to acknowledge that the scene is not only about them. Even if all these things are happening, I know I must never lose my temper, because that just destroys any chance of getting it right.

For these reasons actors will often get angry with me – a form of counter-transference takes place, but the risk of fluctuating popularity is part of the job.

A film set is a potentially disruptive place for actors. Every film crew develops its own way of coping with the challenges of a particular film. A lot of energy is left over between takes – while the tracks are being laid or the make-up applied – it's easy for the actor to start performing to this rather unfocused audience. It's much more difficult to be quietly preparing for the next take. Liz Smith was brilliant in this respect. She'd take her lunch on to the roadside, apparently as Joan Benson, seemingly oblivious to all around her, muttering and singing under her breath. She was always ready for the scene and often her first take was her best.

What is your working method?
I don't have any one method of directing – every actor demands a slightly different approach, a different rhythm. Assuming they have been well cast in the first place, part of the art of directing is to bring them to the boil at the same time. I have often cast actors who have a reputation of being 'difficult', but have rarely found them so. They are often labelled difficult by directors who are afraid to go on a journey with them – which makes them, in turn, afraid, so they behave in such a way as to disguise their fear.

When casting I look for a certain attitude, I suppose, a willingness to fearlessly explore a character – to get lost in a character in quite a childlike way – but I don't necessarily mean a 'method' approach.

Do you ever fear losing control?
If an actor trusts that my only interest is in getting the piece to work as well as possible – and that this is going to require a degree of soul-searching on their part, and they feel that I understand their willingness – control shouldn't come into it. It's a much more private, intense relationship involving a mutual commitment. It shouldn't ever come down to being in charge –

which would be easier in some ways, but in my opinion would mean that the performances wouldn't be as good as they could have been.

As in most areas of film directing, there's a balance to be struck between giving people the freedom to do their best work and keeping them in the world of the story. Most actors understand this; they know that their performances will be used to serve the overall shape of the film. They also know that they might end up on the cutting-room floor! They have much less control than in the theatre. It's one of the givens of film acting. So, accepting that that's the case, there's no point, as the director, in constantly reminding the actors of their status. Much better to encourage them to give more than might be expected, to be surprised by the insights they bring to the characters and the script. If you pretend you know everything, that there is a perfect performance in the director's head and the actors have to achieve some imitation of it, it is not a creative way of working. Besides, I go into the work wanting to be surprised. And given that part of the art of acting is to bring to bear the actor's experience, observation, pain upon the character – to find things in the character which trigger off an 'emotional memory' as Stanislavski called it – inevitably the performance will be fuller than I imagined, because two peoples' insight – the writer's and the actors's – have been brought into contact.

Do you think that directing is about bringing people round to your way of thinking?
There is one level of directing which is simply to do with the art of persuasion, persuading people to get involved in the first place – actors, technicians, financiers, whoever – and then continuing to persuade them to enter fully into this world which we are creating together. And never forgetting that despite the hugeness of the 'operation', it's also a game we are playing, and eventually we want the audience to enter into the game as well.

So, despite the extreme intoxication of all the players, we are simply making something up.

In order to get people intoxicated you have to know what you want; what story you are telling, although not completely of course, or else there'd be nothing to be contributed by them. The people you're collaborating with have to trust that if they give you their commitment and imagination you'll understand and select or amplify their contribution. Indecisiveness at the vital moment is not welcome. It destroys confidence and trust and brings things down to earth. You have to keep things floating somehow.

I never disguise the fact that when I'm directing, I'm pulling together a large number of professional people who will bring highly specialized skills or individual creative energies. I can't do what they do. One of the sublime pleasures of directing is watching people do their jobs, because there comes a time when that's all you can do. Everything is co-ordinated for the take, and suddenly the moment is happening, which is exhilarating.

How carefully did you prepare the shooting of the film with Ian Wilson?
At my first meeting with Ian we mainly talked about colour versus black and white; the idea that because light and form are the most important elements in photography, it is by definition a more natural medium in black and white than colour. The idea was unacceptable to the financiers, and in a way, I think it's a good thing we shot in colour. An old Fenland friend of mine, John Royall, who's a cooper by trade, was talking one night about the old movies he remembered as a young man. 'Course the trouble was, Nick, they weren't in colour' – the thought of making a film which the people of the Fens would regard as old-fashioned would have been persuasion enough.

The discussion about the virtues of black and white photography sparked off a range of ideas which directly and indirectly affected the way we shot the film, above all in our attempt to knock back detail in the image; to render a spareness to the film and to make the colour photography less literal. We tried to make the film appeal to the imagination in some of the ways black and white movies do – to achieve a beauty and expressiveness. So we used various filters combined with strong corrosive lighting in the interiors. Careen Herzog, the designer, also worked to remove colour from backgrounds and strip sets to essentials. The idea was to imagine a particular colour photographed in black and white and then work some of the colour back in.

I found working with Ian both an inspiration and a great pleasure. When we worked through the script scene by scene his input was incalculable, but the interesting thing, looking back, is that although we talked a lot about the films we loved, we never referred to particular films while discussing *Dakota Road*, so the style of shooting emerged solely from the story. Nothing was imposed externally. Once we'd got to know each other, decisions were shared and instantaneous. We had planned very carefully, almost shot by shot, but once I'd prepared the scene with the actors, it was only then that we decided where to put the camera and which lens to use. Then Ian would light. It became a very good routine. I would always rehearse the scene before the actors were made up and costumed, and Ian would then use the time it took them to get ready to light the scene. Usually it worked very smoothly. It also gave the actors a chance to be alone for a while before the take, which is very important.

The fact that Ian both lights and operates helped give our relationship a focus. I liked the fact that it was only Ian I had to consult. As an operator he has the ability to not only frame cinematically and never suggest the obvious choice, but he also manages to transmit energy to a scene. For him lighting and operating are as interdependent as writing and directing are for me.

The day-to-day shooting was the most enjoyable stage in the making of the film. All the things I was most nervous about, like where to put the camera and telling the story visually, evaporated in the doing. Every day there were unforeseen problems, of course, for example the weather would always break when weather continuity was most vital, and occasionally we had underscheduled certain scenes. But even the resolving of these problems became enjoyable, mainly because there was a great sense of support from the crew.

The approach to the look of the film you describe sounds quite unnaturalistic.
I don't think film is naturalistic. A camera does not see things in

the way the human eye does – it's much less sophisticated. The human eye 'pulls focus' continually over a great range, to extremely precise points of concentration – the opposite to the way the camera 'sees'. Which is why the use of framing and camera movement is such an important art, being aware of where the audience will be looking both within the frame and from cut to cut.

It is partly because the human eye is a much more sophisticated instrument than the camera lens that zooming usually feels so peculiar, because it's such a clumsy approximation of what the human eye does naturally. Watching a film is much closer to what we 'see' in a dream than what we see in reality. Many of the devices of film-making have become accepted as 'naturalistic' simply because they form part of a generally accepted convention – but even when film attempts naturalism it is only ever offering a representation of reality.

POST-PRODUCTION

When it came to the editing, did you have it carefully planned?
Of all the stages in the making of *Dakota Road*, the editing was in some ways the most difficult for me. I was too impatient at the beginning – I wanted to force it into shape – I wanted to see it work *immediately*.

But like everything else, time is essential. I think for a while the editor, Bill Diver, felt crowded by me until we'd worked out a routine. Eventually we'd talk through each reel, discuss changes, then I'd leave him to do the work. This meant that for most of the editing period I was sitting in cafés all over the West End, while he cut the film. I'd then return and we'd view the reel in question.

Gradually we found the rhythm of work which was necessary, and I began to get real enjoyment out of seeing the film take shape. In this sense editing is film-making in the literal sense, as different meanings are exposed or created by the individual cuts. The film starts to resonate through the cuts, through the changes in pace and colour. But the musical intensity which is the sign of good film editing does not come easily. Bill said that *Dakota Road* was particularly difficult because you couldn't simply cut out scenes without there being an unforeseen knock-on effect elsewhere in the movie. As this became more apparent through the editing process I actually gained confidence, because it underlined the fact that no single character's point of view ever dominates the overall movement, and unless all the characters were given their beginning, middle and end, the film felt undernourished.

I do, however, find the process of editing quite anachronistic. Cutting-room procedure and technology have not essentially changed since about 1910 (apart from the replacement of cement joins with splicing tape). So it is a slow process and is physically very exhausting for the editor. To recut a scene, even in a very simple way, takes time.

What are the alternatives?
It is an area of innovation. Many directors have cut on video tape for a number of years now, and the most recent development is to cut on laser disc, which means that individual cuts take only a few seconds. There are arguments for and against. But despite the drawbacks, cutting in this way would probably suit my temperament better.

Apart from the technical aspects, the editing forced me to be very honest with the film. I had to cut the film that I'd shot, not the film I'd hoped I'd shot. This was the reason why, as I explained earlier, we cut the film right down on the first cut after the rough assembly – and it didn't work. What I found most interesting was that the editing process often took me back to the script to rediscover my original intentions. Often this was the best way of solving a problem.

How did you approach the music?
I had a very clear sound image of the way the music should work very early in the writing of the script. It was with a reference to 'a single blues guitar – melodic but uneven', that I began the first draft. Music is one of my greatest pleasures in life. I listen to music every day and I usually write with music playing. In most of my theatre work I have used music, usually played live and highly integrated into the production (involving a long association

with composer/violinist Richard Heacock), treating the music as another character in the drama, but also as the scenery, assiduously avoiding using music simply to amplify and generalize emotion – a method, it seems to me, too often employed in film.

I wanted Paul Stacey to compose and play the music because I knew that he had a unique quality. He is primarily a jazz musician, but is extremely versatile. His improvisations are always unpredictable, and given that the *kind* of sound – blues guitar – has been rather overused, in the *Paris, Texas* mode, this was essential.

Paul has other qualities which made him right for *Dakota Road*. I first worked with him as an actor in a production of *Macbeth* I directed for a National Theatre tour of the United States. It was very important that he should approach the music as much as an actor as a musician. He has the ability not just to get inside the mood of a scene, but to get inside the characters' heads as well. So, for me, each cue is remarkably truthful, never simply an imposition of mood or used as a device to crudely amplify emotion.

What stages did you go through?
When it looked likely that the film would go ahead, in about June 1989, Paul was the first person I contacted. He provided a brilliant demo tape overnight, which was his first response to my description of the story and the landscape.

The key *Dakota Road* theme, the 'American' theme, has remained true to that original improvisation. Then much later, in January, just before I went into official pre-production, I went with Paul to the Fens and we spent a couple of days just driving around. In a way he was involved in my first proper location recce. I think his first impressions of that landscape were very important for him.

The next stage was about half-way through the shoot when one weekend we viewed some assembled rushes together on the Steenbeck. Then, after the first assembly, we spent a week in a small studio, basically improvising, and rough-mixed the results into the next cut. It was very clear what worked and what didn't, so by the time we came to the recording session proper, things fell into place quite easily.

I am very pleased with the end result. It's spare and very beautiful with the gradual movement from the electric 'American' theme, with its slightly detached harmonic colour, which seems to capture the essence of Jen's dream of the Americans – who seem so out of reach and yet so ever-present – to the more acoustic themes which predominate at the end of the film. Also, on a purely visceral level, I think the music perfectly suits Ian Wilson's cinematography, which gives the landscape such an oddly American feel.

Why do you use the two K. C. Douglas classic blues tracks?
Partly because they bring a kind of lightness to the film. They allow the audience to enjoy, and are emotionally very open and raw. But also as a kind of tribute to the music which is the root inspiration to Paul's music. I think 'Big Road Blues' for the end credits is the perfect coda to the film, and wonderfully compliments the shot of Amy walking off into the future. However, I wouldn't have felt able to use it without having first infiltrated 'Grievin' Me', which plays in Joan's shop as she sleeps and Amy steals sweets.

In the composition and planning of the music there was always a balance to be struck between individual cues, used for individual dramatic effect, 'pointing' a scene, or giving a scene additional dramatic weight, or cues used to bridge scenes – to build an emotional line between the separate stories – and the overall development and cohesion of the score.

The use of Kenny Wheeler's trumpet was an inspired idea on Paul's part. It introduces a completely contrasting instrumental voice – bringing a colour and melody which is connected to the Church and is unrelated to the predominent American themes. In the last third of the film these themes and colours become interrelated, and a new sound – not directly or subjectively related to Jen – is released.

Throughout the making of the film, what was your relationship with the producers and financiers like?

It's not really accurate to speak of them in the same breath. I had a different relationship with both. The financiers provide the money for the producing company to make the film. So the financiers and the producers also have a relationship, which in the case of Working Title and Channel Four and British Screen goes far beyond *Dakota Road*. So, in a sense, I was the impermanent corner of an ongoing triangle. The arrangement does mean that the financiers, should they so wish, can exert pressure on the director. So at every stage all the decisions taken regarding the film were checked up and down the chain of command.

I think the key to a good relationship with both financiers and producers is to be as open and communicative as possible, at every stage. This was certainly my guiding principle from the outset. After all, the film actually belongs to them. If the director is able to state very clearly what kind of film it is, the people who have raised or are providing the money to make it possible know what kind of film they are going to get. This is why such importance is placed on script development, because the script is regarded as a kind of description, or blueprint of the film. Which is why, incidentally, certain very brilliant film-makers, who don't use conventional scripts, always have incredible difficulty raising money. But that's a separate issue.

So I always tried to keep all the interested parties as much in the picture as I could, asking their advice, and making them aware of all the decisions and choices I was making. For the most part it felt like a genuinely collaborative process. Trouble and interference only happen if the producers or financiers feel they have been misled into expecting something that has not been delivered or if they are unable to accept that the film is what they agreed to. In other words, if there has been a misunderstanding.

Did this happen with Dakota Road?

For the most part, through all the various stages in the making of the film, my relationship with the financiers was very good. Some of the screenings of the various cuts were painful, because I was still trying to find out, for myself, the best rhythm for the film, and was struggling to discover the best balance of the stories. It was therefore quite hard not to get defensive when people offered criticism and comment – although criticism is really *all* that is useful. Sometimes people would find it difficult to articulate a negative feeling or reaction, without being too general. So, often I would try to interpret people's reactions and convert them into a way of making the film better. Often, for instance, people will draw attention to a particular scene as being a 'problem' when the problem scene is the one which comes directly before. Remove or recut the one which comes before and the problem sometimes miraculously disappears.

There was a debate at the end about the music, with people dividing for and against. The word being used was that the film was too 'cold' and that the music wasn't helping. I have tried to put these feelings to positive advantage by going back into the studio with Paul and creating some new themes to complement the original ones, which I think makes the score richer.

I hope that people will see in the film emotions and conflicts they recognize or are living through. For this reason I hope that people who find life difficult – I mean coping with the general business of living, and who feel that so many others find life easy, or at least give the impression of doing so – will respond to the film. I don't think they will find the film bleak, more likely it will make them laugh. It's for those people in particular that I made the film.

So one of the ways that you would counter the accusation of 'bleakness' is by drawing attention to the humour – can you be more specific?
Yes. If you look at the central section of the film, the scenes become much more static and the undercurrent – the subtext if you like – more the driving force. These scenes culminate in the scene between Bernard and Jen in the kitchen, in which he asks her what she wants to do. She reluctantly tells him that she wants to be a hairdresser. He then asks her to cut his hair, although he is almost completely bald. She retaliates by telling him to wash his feet, which he does, using the same bucket of water which featured earlier when Maud cleaned the floor. The scene is concluded with Bernard's physical approach and desperate rejection by Jen.

Jen is always placed in the foreground of the shot, with Bernard in the background. Up until the final confrontation the scene is written with a kind of dead-pan, comic intention, which is the surface texture concealing the much darker currents beneath the surface. In a way it is written as a series of gags and counter gags between the two characters. But when people find out what the outcome is – that Bernard commits suicide soon afterwards – the scene retrospectively gains weight, a vital ingredient in the way the narrative is designed to unfold.

This pattern, the slightly inconsequential handling of the moment-to-moment progress of the film, always placing the interaction of the characters at one remove from the thrust of the narrative, is where I think the humour lies. But I don't claim that I wrote and directed the film to be funny. I did it that way because it felt true to the characters and the Fen people upon whom the characters are based. Also, defining the urge to comedy is very reductive to other possibilities. What I mean is that I won't be disappointed in the least if this scene and others fail to make people laugh, or if people get caught up in the scene in a different way. Maybe they will see only the submerged, religious symbolism of Bernard washing his feet, or will feel with Jen, moment to moment, her acute fear of her father. It comes back to trying to leave a scene open to various interpretations – which I hope is true of the film as a whole.

Sexuality and sexual tension underlie almost every scene in the film. Is this something you intended?
Of course. There's nothing which interests me more – the way peoples' sexuality affects their lives and the lives of others. Although I find it very difficult to say what *Dakota Road* is about – it took me an inordinate amount of time recently to attempt a short synopsis – I suppose the film is, more than anything, about sexuality, both the innocent, positive side and the other, much darker, hidden, unacknowledged side. The film can be seen as a network of forbidden desires – and the damage these can cause, both for the desirer and for the desired. Certainly, and most obviously, Bernard's feelings for Jen and the damage they have caused both of them. Not until she is free of him can she begin to relate to others without aggression, and without great difficulty.

But all the characters are similarly affected, apart from Joan, whose love of God gives her a kind of stability denied the other characters, and Amy, who seems to be taking it all in. There's Alan's feelings for Maud, Douglas's for Raif (which in some ways mirror Bernard's for Jen) and Jen's fantasy about the American pilots. Each is another version of unobtainable desire.

The more I think about it the more I recognize that the film is about unrequited desire and about the fact that sex gets everywhere. But that's not all it's about; it's the undercurrent. Another theme is that most of the characters seem to have lost faith in what they ought to, or appear to, believe in. Again, Joan and Amy are the exceptions.

How important is the marketing of the film?
Vital, but I know it's going to be difficult because it's very hard to find an 'angle' to sell it on. Saying a film is 'about' awakening sexuality or the disintegration of a family is hardly going to bring them flocking!

We live in the age of the marketing of high concepts – films which can be rolled into a phrase, films whose stories are so direct and straightforward that they defy paraphrase – and most films are made only to make money. This has always been the case, since the beginning of cinema: the quality of a film is generally assessed by the quantity of its box-office take. I don't mean to sound anti-popularist, I love some high concept movies and there's nothing I'd like more than to make a film which attracts a large audience. But, I didn't make *Dakota Road* to be anything other than true to itself. This may sound tautologous, but it's the best way I can put it. Maybe this has something to do with it being my first film. But I was very fortunate, at a time when the British Film Industry is on its knees, to find a company who were willing to go along with it – I just hope that it reaches out to as many people as possible, and that it stays with them after they leave the cinema.

Principal Characters

JACOB, an American fighter pilot, stationed at Mildenhall in East Anglia. Aged twenty-eight.

BERNARD CROSS, a Fenland labourer. Early forties.

RAIF BENSON, a railway signalman on the line between Ely and Mildenhall. Early twenties. A Fenman. An orphan. He is physically awkward and inarticulate. Lives with his adoptive grandmother.

JOAN BENSON, Raif's adoptive grandmother. Runs a corner shop and plays the organ in church. Late sixties. A Fenwoman.

JEN CROSS, Bernard's daughter. Aged fifteen.

AMY CROSS, Jen's younger sister. Aged eleven.

MAUD CROSS, married to Bernard. Aged thirty-five. A Fenwoman.

ALAN BRANDON, farmer and landowner. Aged in his fifties.

DOUGLAS STONEA, a vicar. Age: forties.

DAKOTA ROAD

Black screen. Silence. Title: Dakota Road *appears over black. The sound of a single electric blues guitar – the rhythm is slow and the tune slides unevenly but melodically.*

EXTERIOR. AN FIII NUCLEAR BOMBER. DAY
Flying above the sea, the F III enters gradually frame right. It turns suddenly at a very sharp angle and loses height very quickly. The music is the only sound as we cut to . . .

INTERIOR. COCKPIT OF THE FIII. A MOMENT LATER
As the plane is turning we see the pilot, JACOB *in close-up. He is twenty-eight and physically fit. His helmet is emblazoned with the words 'US Air Force'. The music continues, as we see the sky and horizon from* JACOB's *point of view and we cut back to . . .*

EXTERIOR. AN AERIAL VIEW OF THE SEA. A MOMENT LATER
The distant sea rushing towards us – suddenly the aircraft stops its descent, maintaining a constant height. It is now flying at only 300 feet above sea level – the distant water is rushing through the frame. It is spring – sunshine occasionally breaks through the light cloud cover.

INTERIOR. COCKPIT OF THE FIII. A MOMENT LATER
Close-up of JACOB.

EXTERIOR. AERIAL VIEW OF THE LAND. A MOMENT LATER
Below, the criss-crossed patterns of the waterways, fields, railways and roads of East Anglia. The predominant colour of the earth is black.

EXTERIOR. A FIELD. A MOMENT LATER
Directly beneath Jacob's flight path. The low flying F III thunders overhead at two-and-a-half times the speed of sound. BERNARD, *a farm-labourer in his early forties, is driving a tractor, spraying a field with pesticides. He is dressed in a white protective suit. The black peat*

3

*soil is clearly below the level of the river. Bernard's tractor
approaches, systematically covering every inch of the soil. In the
distance, sitting on a dyke above the river bank, are two figures. They
are too far away to be recognizable. We see them in silhouette. In the
other direction, on a slight rise, stands an old farmhouse. Built in the
late eighteenth century, it is a fine building, commanding the
surrounding countryside.*

EXTERIOR. A DYKE ABOVE THE RIVER BANK. A MOMENT
LATER

JEN, *Bernard's elder daughter, aged fifteen, and* RAIF *(early
twenties), a signalman on the railway between Ely and Lakenheath,
are about to make love on the dyke above the river bank. Both of them
still have most of their clothes on. Jen's flying jacket (a cheap imitation
of the one we saw* JACOB *wearing) is lying discarded beside them. On
it are various American flying insignia, including the stars and stripes.
In the background, the field where* BERNARD *is working. He is visible
in the distance. On the river bank is Raif's fishing rod and tackle,
obviously unattended. Dead fish float past. Behind them there is a
railway bridge.*
RAIF: Love you.
JEN: Go on then . . .
RAIF: Right.

4

EXTERIOR. ALAN BRANDON'S FARM HOUSE. A MOMENT
LATER
ALAN BRANDON, *a farmer and landowner in his fifties, can be seen
standing at the window of his upstairs study. He is looking out
across the fen through a mounted telescope.*

INTERIOR. ALAN BRANDON'S STUDY. A MOMENT LATER
*It is a beautifully proportioned room, very sparsely decorated, and
painted white. The effect is austere. On the mantelpiece there is a
single photograph of his dead wife, beside it a small vase of flowers
and a crucifix. There is the sound of a grandfather clock – the steady
tick-tock echoes through the house. There is a feeling of loneliness and
emptiness.* ALAN *is looking out through the mounted telescope. We see*
BERNARD *spraying from his point of view.* ALAN *pans around and
focuses on* JEN *and* RAIF.

EXTERIOR. A DYKE ABOVE THE RIVER BANK. A MOMENT
LATER
RAIF *and* JEN *are now lying on the dyke beside the river.*
JEN: Raif.
RAIF: What?
JEN: Go on then!
RAIF: (*Struggling*) Right. (RAIF *is obviously experiencing
    considerable difficulty.*)
JEN: What are you doing, then?
RAIF: Hang on a minute.

INTERIOR/EXTERIOR. ALAN BRANDON'S STUDY. A MOMENT
LATER
Through Alan's telescope we see RAIF *and* JEN *making love. In the
background,* BERNARD *driving the tractor.* ALAN *is obviously excited
by what he sees, and zooms in slightly on the couple.*

EXTERIOR. THE DYKE ABOVE THE RIVER BANK. A MOMENT
LATER
JEN *and* RAIF *making love.*
JEN: Raif.
RAIF: What?

5

JEN: Go *careful*.
RAIF: Right.
    (RAIF *has an orgasm*.)

INTERIOR. ALAN BRANDON'S FARMHOUSE. A MOMENT LATER
ALAN *is still watching the scene through his telescope. He lifts his
head.*

EXTERIOR. THE RIVER BANK. A SHORT TIME LATER
RAIF *is sitting on the top of the dyke, separate from* JEN, *who is below
him. He is looking at some dead fish floating past. The sound of a
train. It passes over the bridge. The sound of the train is amplified as it
crosses the bridge.*

6

JEN: Raif, what you done?
  (*Pause.*)
RAIF: Look at 'em.
  (JEN *climbs up the bank.*)
JEN: What you on about?
  (*A shot of* BERNARD *spraying from* RAIF's *point of view.*)
RAIF: Them fish . . . That's your Dad's doing . . . He's killed 'em
  with his spraying. That he has . . .
JEN: That's not his. That's Mr Brandon's pesticide, what he's
  spraying. That's whose it is – anyway Raif, you promised to
  go careful . . .
RAIF: I'll *marry* you – so there you go . . .
JEN: I won't marry you, nor no one – so shut your noise . . .

INTERIOR/EXTERIOR. THE CHURCH. THE SAME DAY
*A large church, like many in East Anglia, built with the wealth
generated by the Wool Trade. There is a slightly dilapidated feel – the
church is obviously short of funds for basic repair work. There is also
the feeling that the church is very under-attended. There are very few
hymnals and prayer books on the shelves by the main entrance. Shafts
of early-evening sunlight filter through stain glass windows and strike
the empty pews diagonally.* JOAN BENSON, *the village shop keeper, a
woman in her late sixties, is practising the organ (which she plays for
services). We can only see her back – she is positioned to the left of the
altar in the aisle. As she plays, she is singing a Charles Wesley hymn
loudly and unselfconsciously.*
JOAN: (*Singing*) Jesus Lord, we look to Thee,
      Let us in Thy name agree;
      Show Thyself the Prince of Peace;
      Bid our jarring conflicts cease.

      Let us for each other care,
      Each the other's burden bear,
      To Thy Church the pattern give,
      Show how true believers live.

INTERIOR. THE CHURCH VESTRY. A MOMENT LATER
The sound of JOAN's *singing continues. Hanging on the walls are*

7

vestments, and on shelves there are sacramental chalices and candlesticks. The room is illustrated by a single shaft of sunlight from a narrow arched window. DOUGLAS STONEA, *a vicar in his fifties, is sitting at an old oak table with a chess set in front of him, laid out for the beginning of a game. He is looking at a severe, Lutheran crucifix, positioned separately from the other objects in the vestry. The crucifix depicts Christ in appalling agony.* DOUGLAS *is fit-looking and has a rather serious and intimidating appearance. He is wearing an old black suit and dog-collar. On another wall there are two photographs of* RAIF, *one taken when he was much younger, in which* DOUGLAS *is holding him above his head.* . . . *In the other, which is more recent (maybe two years before),* RAIF *is dressed in a surplus for serving in church services. A shaft of sunlight strikes the crucifix directly, giving it a rather odd, mysterious illumination. A cloud crosses the sun. The light on the crucifix dims for a moment.* DOUGLAS *looks away. The sunlight returns.* JOAN's *singing continues.*

INTERIOR. THE CHURCH. A MOMENT LATER
JOAN *has stopped singing now. She looks tired and unwell. She sits slumped forward over the keyboard.* DOUGLAS *has come up behind her without seeing him.*
DOUGLAS: I was expecting Raif. Have you seen him?
JOAN: Not since this morning. 'Spect he's fishing.
DOUGLAS: I see . . . You should be resting.
JOAN: You say that, but without me you'd never manage.
DOUGLAS: True enough.
　　　(*As we see* DOUGLAS *leave, we hear an* F111 *thunder overhead.*)

EXTERIOR. THE SKY A MOMENT LATER
An F111 *flies overhead.*

EXTERIOR. THE RIVER BANK. A MOMENT LATER
RAIF *and* JEN. *The sound of the* F111 *is deafening.*
JEN: (*Shouts*) Take me away!
　　　(*She waves at the sky with both arms.*)
RAIF: Don't start that again.
JEN: Eh, Raif, what'd you think it's like?
RAIF: What?

8

JEN: Up there . . . What d'you think *he's* like?
    (*She points to the sky.*)
RAIF: Don't start that again . . .
    (*They move together, pretending to fight.*)

INTERIOR F I I I. JACOB'S COCKPIT. A MOMENT LATER
JACOB'*s face in close-up. He looks very tired – returning after a
training exercise. The sound of landing instructions over Jacob's radio.
American accents.*

EXTERIOR. THE US AIRBASE. A MOMENT LATER
Jacob's F I I I lands.

EXTERIOR. A FIELD. A SHORT WHILE LATER
BERNARD *has nearly finished spraying the field. He is closer now to*
RAIF *and* JEN *who are clearly visible, mock-fighting on the dyke
above the river bank.*

EXTERIOR. THE DYKE ABOVE THE RIVER BANK. A MOMENT
LATER
RAIF *and* JEN. BERNARD *driving the tractor in the background.*
RAIF: You reckon your Dad can see us?
JEN: Bloody hope not.
RAIF: Let's get out of it.
(*They quickly descend the dyke, out of sight of* BERNARD.)

EXTERIOR. THE RIVER BANK. A SHORT WHILE LATER
In the distance, DOUGLAS *can see Raif's discarded fishing equipment.*
He can't see RAIF *and* JEN. *He thinks something must have happened*
to RAIF. *He hurries along the river bank.*

EXTERIOR. BERNARD'S HOUSE. LATER THE SAME DAY
A very isolated tied cottage, surrounded by fields. Top of next scene is
heard in voice-over.

INTERIOR. BERNARD'S HOUSE. AMY AND JEN'S ROOM. THE SAME DAY

The walls of the small room are covered with pictures, cut out of magazines, of American airmen and aircraft. There are also a few film posters – including one for Top Gun. AMY, *Bernard's younger daughter, aged eleven, is applying lipstick. She is looking into a small mirror, behind which is a large American flag. Hold for a few moments. We hear* MAUD, *Bernard's wife, thirty-five, shouting from another room. Camera holds on* AMY, *until* MAUD *enters.*

MAUD: (*Voice-over*) Amy! (*Pause.*) Amy! Where's Jen?

AMY: What?

MAUD: (*Voice-over*) Where's your sister?

AMY: Don't know.

    (MAUD *enters the bedroom.*)

MAUD: Amy! . . . I'm talking to you . . . What *are* you doing?
    (*She snatches the lipstick.*)
    That's mine.

AMY: Jen gave it to me.

MAUD: Well, Jen had no business giving it to you.
    (*She slaps her wrist, then wipes the lipstick from her lips roughly.*)

AMY: Shouldn't hit.

MAUD: It were only a slap.

AMY: Shouldn't slap, then.
    (AMY *is about to cry.*)

MAUD: Don't cry. And say sorry. (*Pause.*) I said say sorry.
    (*Pause.*)

AMY: Sorry.
    (MAUD *starts to leave.*)

AMY: (*Angry*) I *do* know where Jen is. But I'm not telling you.

EXTERIOR. THE RIVER BANK. THE SAME DAY

RAIF *has pushed* JEN *down. He is on top of her. They are both still only partially dressed. A view of the sky from* JEN's *point of view. The sound of* RAIF *getting passionate again. Suddenly* DOUGLAS *is above her, filling the frame.*

JEN: Raif! Raif!
    (JEN *pushes* RAIF *off her.*)

RAIF: What?
>(RAIF *sees* DOUGLAS. DOUGLAS *and* RAIF *stare at each other for a moment.* DOUGLAS, *in a state of shock, hurries away*.)

RAIF: Oh, God . . .

JEN: He don't even know the facts o' life, I shouldn't wonder.

RAIF: Don't know what you're laughing at, Jen . . . You'll get me in no end of trouble.

JEN: He's not your *Dad*, Raif . . .

RAIF: You don't know nothing.

JEN: Well, at least I'm not an *orphan*.

RAIF: Shut up, Jen . . .

JEN: Don't tell *me* to shut up.

RAIF: Must be getting back, anyroad.

JEN: Why?

RAIF: Have to, *now* . . . Fish is all dead, anyway, I reckon . . .

JEN: We didn't come here for the fishing, Raif . . .

RAIF: . . . and that's your Dad's doing . . . Killed our river, he has . . .

JEN: Yeah, well he'll kill *you* if he finds out – 'cause I'm under age, Raif Benson . . .

RAIF: Come on.

INTERIOR/EXTERIOR. A SHED. THE SAME DAY
BERNARD *has finished work. He drives the tractor into a shed.*

EXTERIOR. AN UNLEVELLED ROAD. LATER THE SAME DAY
BERNARD *has begun to walk home, down a small track. The sound of a car.* ALAN BRANDON *is driving his Range Rover down the track towards* BERNARD. BERNARD *stops walking.* ALAN BRANDON *draws up beside him.*

ALAN: Bernard!

BERNARD: Mr Brandon.

ALAN: I've been looking for you.

BERNARD: Oh yes, Mr Brandon.

ALAN: Which way are you heading?

BERNARD: Just knocked off. So I'm off home.

ALAN: Bit early to knock off, isn't it?

BERNARD: That's gone four-thirty, Mr Brandon.

ALAN: Of course it has. I wasn't suggesting anything. I'm just
surprised it's so late already . . . Must be these long evenings
. . . Have you time for a talk?
BERNARD: Course I have.
(ALAN *opens the car door.* BERNARD *starts to get in.*)
Wait a minute.
(*He places an old towel over the seat.* BERNARD *gets in.*)

EXTERIOR. THE ROADSIDE. LATER THE SAME DAY
ALAN *has driven the car a short distance, off the track, on to the edge
of a field, facing the railway track. To one side a drainage channel
with a pumping station, taking water through to the river.*
ALAN: How long has it been?
BERNARD: What's that, Mr Brandon.
ALAN: Long time, eh Bernard?
BERNARD: Yup.
(*Pause.*)

ALAN: Things are changing, Bernard.

BERNARD: You what?

ALAN: Oh nothing. (*Pause.*) Did you know that Ousey Hill Road has a new name?

BERNARD: Didn't know that, Mr Brandon.

ALAN: Indeed. They call it Dakota Road now. What do you think of that?

BERNARD: That's still Ousey Hill Road to me. Mind you, there never were much of a hill . . . (*He laughs.*)

ALAN: You see, Bernard, absolutely nothing is fixed in life . . . One thing gives way to another . . .

BERNARD: You got a point there, Mr Brandon.

ALAN: How's your wife, these days?

BERNARD: Not too bad.

ALAN: Lovely woman . . . How's your daughter? Jennifer isn't it?

BERNARD: Not too bad, thank you . . . And Amy, me youngest, she i'n't too bad, neither. Thank you for asking.

ALAN: So how old is she now? Jennifer?

BERNARD: Fifteen.

ALAN: Aha! That's when all the trouble starts.

BERNARD: What?

ALAN: I think I saw her today.

BERNARD: She i'n't got no job yet, worst luck.

ALAN: Things are getting very difficult . . . Lovely girl . . .

BERNARD: Is there anything else you were wanting, Mr Brandon? 'Cause I'd best be getting along home, now, if it's all the same to you.

ALAN: Things are *always* changing – things are getting hard. Even here.

BERNARD: Things don't change that easy in my eyes . . . Well, I'll be off then.
(*He gets out of the car.*)

ALAN: Goodnight, Bernard.

BERNARD: Goodnight, Mr Brandon.
(*He starts up the engine of his car.* BERNARD *has started to walk away*.)

ALAN: (*Calling after him*) Bernard?

BERNARD: Yup.

ALAN: What job are you on tomorrow?
BERNARD: Still be spraying.
ALAN: I see. Goodnight.
BERNARD: Goodnight to you.
> (BERNARD *turns and walks away.* ALAN *drives off.*)

EXTERIOR. NEAR RAIF'S SIGNALBOX. LATER THE SAME DAY
RAIF *and* JEN. RAIF *is dropping off his fishing tackle. A signalman is visible.*
RAIF: See you tomorrow, then.
JEN: If you're lucky.
> (*She walks off.*)

EXTERIOR. OUTSIDE JOAN BENSON'S CORNER SHOP. THE
SAME DAY
JOAN *is attending to her flowerbed. The door to the general store is open. The shop looks under-stocked and slightly anachronistic. The flowerbeds are overcrowded with a great variety of very colourful flowers. A black cat is sitting on the window-sill.* DOUGLAS *is standing over* JOAN.
DOUGLAS: (*Angry*) The girl is only fifteen years old. In the eyes of both the Church and the Law what they are doing is *wrong*.
JOAN: Right you are . . . D'you want some flowers while you're here . . .? Old church could do with a little cheering up . . .
> (RAIF *approaching in long shot. Camera stays with him.*)
DOUGLAS: I ask you to *look* to him.
JOAN: You can look to him yourself – 'cause he's just coming.
DOUGLAS: No. I'll leave it to you. That's best.
> (DOUGLAS *leaves.* RAIF *sits down on a seat beside the flowerbed. A silence.*)
JOAN: So what you been up to?
RAIF: Fishing.
JOAN: What else?
RAIF: You know what else, 'cause Mr Stonea just told you what else . . .
JOAN: Well then, just go careful.
RAIF: Right.
JOAN: Otherwise you'll end up in a state, like your mother did –

and next time I won't be here to help out.
RAIF: Right.
JOAN: 'Spect you're hungry.
RAIF: Right.
JOAN: Come on then.
RAIF: Right.

INTERIOR. MAUD'S KITCHEN. LATER THE SAME DAY
The decor of the kitchen–living room is old-fashioned and not particularly charming or tasteful. However, the table is made of old oak, as are the sideboards. There are many pieces of china, on every available surface, and a bunch of cut daffodils in a vase on the sideboard. MAUD *is preparing supper, fishfingers and mashed potatoes.* AMY *is sitting at the table.*

EXTERIOR/INTERIOR. BERNARD'S HOUSE. A MOMENT LATER
BERNARD *kicking the mud from his boots. Having done so, he meticulously places them side by side inside the front door. He then removes his protective clothing – which he hangs up neatly.*

INTERIOR. MAUD'S KITCHEN. A MOMENT LATER
BERNARD *is sitting at the table next to* AMY. *He says nothing.* AMY's *face still looks tear-stained.* MAUD *is peeling potatoes. She looks at* BERNARD. BERNARD *ignores her.* BERNARD *looks at* AMY.
BERNARD: What's up with you?
AMY: She hit me.
BERNARD: Come 'ere.
AMY: What for?
BERNARD: Come 'ere.
    (AMY *goes to him.*)
    What's that you got?
    (*She gives him the lipstick. He puts lipstick roughly around his mouth. He laughs. He looks like a clown.* AMY *laughs.*)

EXTERIOR. THE EDGE OF A DRAINAGE CHANNEL. LATER THE SAME EVENING
JEN *is sitting alone. It's getting dark. An* F111 *flies overhead. She points a stick at the plane, and pretends to shoot it. It suddenly flies at*

a sharp angle, as if evading her. She looks away – for a moment she is genuinely frightened that she has *shot it down.* JEN *pokes a dying fish with the stick, as we cut to . . .*

INTERIOR. MAUD'S KITCHEN. LATER THE SAME EVENING
Close-up of MAUD *cooking fishfingers. Time lapse. The family is sitting at the table.* JEN *picks at her fishfingers.*
BERNARD: Don't pick.
JEN: What you kill all them fish for?
BERNARD: What?
JEN: You know, you killed 'em with that spraying o' yours. You should be ashamed.
MAUD: Don't talk to your father like that.
   (JEN *looks at the lipstick on* BERNARD's *face.*)
JEN: He looks soft.
   (*She gets up. Leaves the room.*)

INTERIOR. JEN AND AMY'S BEDROOM. NIGHT
AMY *is in bed.* JEN *is sitting on the edge of her bed looking out of the window. Silence. The room is very dark.*
AMY: Jen?
JEN: What?
AMY: You know.
JEN: What?
AMY: Do it?
JEN: Yup.
   (*Pause.*)
AMY: Well?
JEN: What?
AMY: What's it like then?
JEN: Mind your own . . .
AMY: You said you'd tell me if you done it . . .
JEN: You got to wait.
AMY: What?
JEN: You got to wait till you're old enough to find out for yourself.
AMY: Don't want to.
JEN: Shut up.
   (*Slight pause.*)

18

AMY: I hate you.
JEN: Good.

INTERIOR. MAUD'S KITCHEN. LATER THE SAME NIGHT
BERNARD *is sitting alone. He picks up his boots which he has put on
the table in front of him and starts to clean them. He scrapes the mud
off first – ready to polish them.*
MAUD: (*Voice-over*) Bernard! What *are* you doing?

INTERIOR. JEN AND AMY'S ROOM. NIGHT. A MOMENT LATER
In the darkness. JEN *is listening at the door, which she is holding
slightly open. A thin shaft of light, from Maud's bedroom along the
short corridor, falls across her face. The sound of* BERNARD *cleaning
his boots.*
MAUD: (*From her bedroom*) Bernard! Won't you come to bed?

INTERIOR. MAUD'S KITCHEN. NIGHT. A MOMENT LATER
BERNARD *stops cleaning his boots. He leaves the kitchen, turning off
the light as he goes.*

INTERIOR. JEN AND AMY'S ROOM. NIGHT. A FEW MOMENTS
LATER
JEN *is still listening at the partly open door. The sound of* BERNARD
coming up the stairs. JEN *closes the door. He stands still for a few
moments. He then continues along the corridor to his bedroom.*

INTERIOR. MAUD'S BEDROOM. NIGHT
MAUD *is already in bed. She is sitting up with a bedside light on. Her
clothes are carefully laid out on a bedside chair.* BERNARD *comes in
and stands at the end of the bed. Pause.*
MAUD: What's wrong with you, Bernard? You've hardly said a
   word all night . . .

INTERIOR. JEN AND AMY'S BEDROOM. A MOMENT LATER
JEN *opens the door again and creeps out on to the corridor.*

INTERIOR. MAUD'S BEDROOM. A MOMENT LATER
MAUD: Bernard? I'm speaking to you . . .

BERNARD: (*Quietly*) Alan Brandon's up to something.

INTERIOR. THE CORRIDOR. NIGHT. A MOMENT LATER
JEN *listens intently to their conversation. It is very dark, but her face is quite visible, animated by fear and curiosity as she listens.*

MAUD: (*Voice-over*) Alan Brandon's always up to something . . .
    So what's he said?

BERNARD: (*Voice-over*) . . . And I don't like your shouting at Jen
    . . . Don't like it, right?

MAUD: (*Voice-over*) What's he said, Bernard?

BERNARD: (*Voice-over*) . . . And Jen's right about them
    pesticides. River's dead – as good as . . .

MAUD: (*Voice-over*) Well, you should damned well stick up for
    yourself. That's not just *his* river . . . Anyway, what's he
    said?

BERNARD: (*Voice-over*) Nothing – he said nothing . . . It's the way
    he said it . . .

MAUD: (*Voice-over*) What's got into you, Bernard Cross . . .
    Talking in riddles . . . I think Jen's got a point – you *are*
    going soft in the head.

BERNARD: (*Voice-over. Suddenly very angry.*) I'm not soft in the
    head – you ask – I fucking tell you . . . You shouldn't talk to
    Jen like that – you shouldn't hit my Amy . . . I don't like it,
    right?

MAUD: (*Voice-over*) Don't shout at me . . . *Your* Amy!

BERNARD: (*Voice-over*) I'll fucking shout . . . I do what I fucking
    like . . .
    (*The camera remains on* JEN's *face in close-up. The sound of*
    BERNARD's *violence. He storms out of the room.*)

INTERIOR. THE CORRIDOR. NIGHT. A MOMENT LATER
JEN *hears* BERNARD *coming. She quickly returns to her room.*
BERNARD *walks through the frame.*

INTERIOR. THE KITCHEN. NIGHT. A MOMENT LATER
In darkness BERNARD *stands by the table. He continues to polish his
boots.*

INTERIOR. MAUD'S BEDROOM. A MOMENT LATER
MAUD *sits alone in the bed. She turns the light off. The sound of*
BERNARD *cleaning his boots continues.*

INTERIOR. JEN AND AMY'S BEDROOM. LATER THE SAME
NIGHT
JEN *is lying in bed, wide awake. We head the sound of* BERNARD
*cleaning his boots – which continues throughout the scene. She looks
across at* AMY, *who is still asleep.*
JEN: Amy? (*Pause.*) Amy? Are you asleep? I'll tell you if you like
. . . You know? What it were like . . . I'll tell you all about it.
(*Silence.* AMY *sleeps.* JEN *gets into Amy's bed.* AMY *stirs.*)
But there i'n't much to tell.
(*She curls around* AMY. *They both sleep.*)

EXTERIOR. OUTSIDE THE HIGH SECURITY FENCE
SURROUNDING THE US AIRBASE AT MILDENHALL. EARLY
MORNING
In the foreground a road sign: 'DAKOTA ROAD'. *In the distance the
aerial runway. There are no people. The aircraft are lined up. Music.
A single F111 takes off down the runway.*

INTERIOR. AMY AND JEN'S BEDROOM. EARLY MORNING
A shot of the aircraft on Jen's wall. AMY *and* JEN *sleeping together.
The sound of an F111 passing overhead.* JEN *stirs in her sleep.* AMY
wakes up.
AMY: Get off.

EXTERIOR. OUTSIDE RAIF'S SIGNALBOX. THE SAME
MORNING
RAIF *is sweeping up. He is surprised by* DOUGLAS, *who has come up
behind him.*
DOUGLAS: (*Smiling*) Raif . . . About yesterday . . . I'm not going
to *report* you for what happened.
RAIF: Report?
DOUGLAS: As long as it doesn't happen again, that is.
RAIF: Right.
DOUGLAS: The reason I'm hard on you is because I *care* for you.

You know that, don't you?

RAIF: Right you are.

DOUGLAS: I miss you, around the church, I mean . . . Take care now.

(RAIF *nods.* DOUGLAS *walks down the road towards the church.*)

EXTERIOR. THE RAILWAY BRIDGE OVER THE RIVER. THE SAME MORNING
BERNARD *is alone on the railway bridge. A shot of his very clean boots. He looks over the side into the water.*

INTERIOR. RAIF'S SIGNALBOX. THE SAME MORNING
RAIF *checks the clock against the timetable. He leaves the signalbox to close the gates to traffic.*

EXTERIOR. THE RAILWAY BRIDGE. THE SAME MORNING
BERNARD *is between the rails. He puts his ear to the tracks.*

EXTERIOR. RAIF'S RAILWAY CROSSING. A MOMENT LATER
A train travels through the frame. A great noise.

EXTERIOR. THE RAILWAY BRIDGE ACROSS THE RIVER. A MOMENT LATER
BERNARD *is still on the tracks. The oncoming train is visible in the distance. The sound of the tracks tightening.*

EXTERIOR. THE RAILWAY BRIDGE OVER THE RIVER. A FEW MOMENTS LATER
The train travelling over the bridge. BERNARD *is not in sight. The last carriage clears the centre of the bridge, revealing* BERNARD. *He is looking down into the water.*

INTERIOR. THE CHURCH. DAY. LATER THE SAME MORNING
The church is empty except for ALAN BRANDON *who is looking at a plaque on the wall. The plaque is in memory of his wife, Elizabeth Brandon. The plaque looks very new in comparison to the others – probably the only one erected in living memory. There are several plaques, all much older, which commemorate other members of the*

*Brandon family, including Alan's father, William Brandon. The
church is full of light, which the white-washed walls seem to reflect
and magnify. The sound of* DOUGLAS *entering the church by the main
gate. On hearing him* ALAN *kneels and takes up the posture of prayer.*
DOUGLAS *sees him and approaches him very quietly.* DOUGLAS *taps*
ALAN *on the shoulder, very gently.* ALAN *pretends to be surprised.*
DOUGLAS *speaks in a low reverential whisper.*

DOUGLAS: Sorry to disturb you Alan, but I must thank you for
    your generous gift . . .
    (ALAN *stands up.*)
ALAN: May I have a word?

EXTERIOR. OUTSIDE THE CHURCH. THE SAME MORNING
JOAN *approaches the church. She is carrying huge bunches of freshly
cut flowers.*

INTERIOR. THE CHURCH. A FEW MOMENTS LATER
DOUGLAS *and* ALAN *talking, on the other side of the church, from*
JOAN'*s point of view. They look conspiratorial. We follow her on her
way to the altar to arrange the flowers. She is singing under her breath.*

INTERIOR. ANOTHER PART OF THE CHURCH. A SHORT
WHILE LATER
JOAN *arranges the flowers.* ALAN *and* DOUGLAS *are still talking. We
see them from* JOAN'*s point of view. She breaks off from her flower-
arranging and walks towards them. They stop speaking as they notice*
JOAN *approaching.*

ALAN: Mrs Benson! May I say how *charming* the flowers look.
    Such a beautiful contribution.
JOAN: I come for more vases, Mr Stonea.
DOUGLAS: Right you are.
JOAN: (*To* ALAN) Contribution, you say? Them's God's flowers,
    to start out, and what's more, it's flowers and singing what
    gives interest to worship – i'n't that right, Mr Stonea?
DOUGLAS: Vases! Right! (*To* ALAN) Alan, why don't we go into
    the vestry – it'll be quieter in there.
    (JOAN *walks back to the altar.* DOUGLAS *and* ALAN *walk
    towards the vestry.*)

23

ALAN: (*Whispering*) We should have pointed out to her that if it
wasn't for *my* contribution, God's house wouldn't have a roof.
(DOUGLAS *leads him into the vestry.*)
DOUGLAS: (*Whispering*) She's not well, Alan.

INTERIOR. MAUD'S KITCHEN. SOME TIME LATER
MAUD *is scrubbing the floor, on her hands and knees.* JEN *and* AMY
sitting at the table. Both eating toast. JEN *is wearing a very broken-
down leather outfit.* AMY *imitates the way* JEN *eats.* JEN *is annoyed at
this.*
MAUD: Just look at you. Who d'you think you are . . .
(MAUD *doesn't stop washing the floor as she speaks.* AMY *laughs.*)
And I don't know what you find so damned funny.

(*Silence.* MAUD *continues to clean the floor.*)

JEN: I'm going out.

MAUD: Well, you can take her with you.

JEN: Don't have to.

MAUD: You do.

AMY: (*Whispering*) Do have to.

JEN: (*To* MAUD) Anything to get away from you. (*To* AMY) Come
    on then, if you have to.

    (AMY *and* JEN *leave. As* AMY *goes out of the door, she looks
    back momentarily and catches* MAUD's *eye.*)

EXTERIOR. OUTSIDE ALAN BRANDON'S HOUSE. THE SAME
DAY

BERNARD *is outside Alan's front door. He knocks.* ALAN *opens the
door immediately.*

ALAN: Ah, Bernard, just the man. I wanted to talk to you.

BERNARD: My Jen and my Maud reckon on it not being no good –
    spraying all these old pesticides . . . Said I ought to say it to
    you straight, 'cause it's been on my mind – if you see what I
    mean.

ALAN: Has it just?

BERNARD: It has – and on the minds of others.

ALAN: I see. (*Slight pause. Suddenly very abrupt*) What job are you
    on tomorrow?

BERNARD: Clearing twelve-foot drain.

ALAN: I see. I'll have a word with you in the morning.

    (*He shuts the door abruptly.*)

INTERIOR. A BARN. THE SAME DAY

JEN, AMY *and* RAIF.

RAIF: (*Indicating* AMY) What's she doing?

AMY: She's got to take me with her. (*Long pause.*)

RAIF: You like it?

JEN: What?

RAIF: What we done yesterday.

JEN: No.

    (AMY *laughs.*)

    Shut up, Amy.

(*Pause.*)

RAIF: Why?

JEN: What?

RAIF: Why didn't you like it?

JEN: Shan't say . . . Anyway, Raif, you promised to go careful.
(*Pause.*)

RAIF: Well, we can't do it no more.

JEN: What?

RAIF: You're too young for it . . . Get me into trouble . . . Trouble
with the law, I mean . . . Mr Stonea said he'd report me if I
done it again.

JEN: I'm going then.

RAIF: Don't go.

JEN: I'm going. You won't see me no more.
(JEN *starts to leave.*)
Amy!

RAIF: I got to see you . . . 'Cause I love you and I want to marry
you, like what I said.

JEN: Well, I don't want to marry no one. Least of all you, 'cause I
don't even *like* you.

RAIF: What?

JEN: 'Cause you're scared . . .

RAIF: Not scared.

JEN: Are so.

RAIF: Not.

JEN: I'm going. Come on, Amy – we're going.
(*They leave.*)

EXTERIOR. OUTSIDE THE PERIMETER FENCE. US AIRBASE.
THE SAME DAY

JEN *and* AMY *are walking along the edge of the high-security fence. As
they talk, they look across at the aircraft and airmen in the distance.
Some of the following dialogue we hear in voice-over as we see the
American activities.*

AMY: So, what happened?

JEN: There was this, like, school – only it were a school for men,
who fly them planes, like them here.

AMY: What, Americans?

26

JEN: 'Course, stupid.
AMY: What's he like?
JEN: Who?
AMY: The man in the film.
JEN: He rides a motorbike.
AMY: Does he look like Raif?
JEN: *No*. Raif i'n't *sexy*, like *him*.
AMY: Raif *is* sexy, though.
JEN: Shut up, Amy.
    (*Slight pause. They walk in silence for a while.*)

EXTERIOR. BY THE RIVER. LATER THE SAME AFTERNOON
JEN *is cutting* AMY's *hair*.
JEN: Sit still.
    (*The sound of an F111 flying overhead.*)

EXTERIOR. BERNARD'S HOUSE. THE SAME EVENING
MAUD *is sitting on a kitchen chair, reading a romantic novel.*
BERNARD *is sitting outside the front door, cleaning his boots again.*
BERNARD: (*Proudly*) I told him.
MAUD: Did you, Bernard? What, 'bout the spraying?
BERNARD: That's right.
MAUD: And?
BERNARD: He didn't like it.
MAUD: 'Course he didn't. What did he say?
BERNARD: Not a lot. (*Anxiously, to himself*) Always done twelve
    foot. Time of year.
MAUD: What you on about?
BERNARD: He said, what was I doing tomorrow?
    (JEN *and* AMY *approach the house.*)
    Here they come.
MAUD: About time too.
BERNARD: I only said it 'cause Jen said to say it.
MAUD: *I* told you to say it. It were *me*.
BERNARD: I done it for *Jen*. Not you.
MAUD: All right.
    (JEN *and* AMY *go into the house.* MAUD *sees* AMY's *new haircut.*)
    What *have* you done?
BERNARD: Leave her be.
MAUD: Bernard!

INTERIOR. THE SITTING ROOM. BERNARD'S HOUSE. THE
SAME DAY
JEN *and* AMY *are watching television, a single blues guitar fills the
frame – the volume is very loud.* BERNARD *enters.*
BERNARD: (*To* AMY) Looks *all right*. (*To* JEN) I told him.
JEN: What *you* on about?
BERNARD: (*Pleased*) I told Alan Brandon what you said to say to
    him, 'bout the spraying.
JEN: I don't care.

INTERIOR. JOAN'S HOUSE. THE SITTING ROOM. THE SAME
EVENING
JOAN *and* RAIF *are sitting together watching television, the same*

programme that JEN *and* AMY *were watching. The volume is very
low. The room is very cluttered and quite dirty.*
JOAN: (*Sleepily*) What's up with you?
RAIF: She don't want me no more.
JOAN: (*Going to sleep*) That's probably for the best. Don't you
worry 'bout nothing . . .

INTERIOR. JOAN'S BEDROOM. LATER THE SAME NIGHT
The room is very simply furnished. JOAN *is preparing for bed.*

INTERIOR. RAIF'S BEDROOM. NIGHT
Close-up of RAIF *asleep. He is having a nightmare. His face contorts.*

INTERIOR. JOAN'S BEDROOM. NIGHT
JOAN *has got into bed. We hear* RAIF *scream.*

INTERIOR. RAIF'S BEDROOM. NIGHT
A shot of Raif's window from RAIF'*s point of view. The window is
partly open. The curtain moves in the breeze.* JOAN *is by his bedside.*
RAIF: What's he want?

JOAN: Who?

RAIF: Mr Stonea?

JOAN: What d'you mean?

RAIF: What's he *want*.

JOAN: He loves you like a father – 'cause he i'n't got a child . . .

RAIF: Well, I don't love him.

JOAN: Don't worry about *him* . . . Don't you worry 'bout
     nothing . . .

RAIF: Don't love him at all . . . I love Jen Cross . . .

JOAN: I know you do. (*Slight pause.*) Raif?

RAIF: What?

JOAN: What were it like?

RAIF: What?

JOAN: What were it like? With Jen Cross, by the river?
     (*Pause.*)

RAIF: It were nice.

JOAN: I bet it were.

RAIF: It were real nice.
     (*Pause.*)

JOAN: Were it? Now you sleep.

RAIF: All right then.

JOAN: That's it.
     (*She kisses him. He sleeps.*)

EXTERIOR. A DRAINAGE CHANNEL. DAY

BERNARD *is clearing the drain of debris (including dead fish – large
bloated bream). He is in a boat.* ALAN, *on foot, shouts from the other
side of the drain.*

ALAN: Bernard . . . I've been looking for you.

BERNARD: You have, Mr Brandon?

ALAN: How are you today?
     (BERNARD *nods.*)
     I'm going to have to lay you off, Bernard.

BERNARD: Yup.

ALAN: You've been here a long time. So, it's hard for me, you
     understand that, don't you? Your complaint about the
     pesticides, Bernard – you understand I take that very
     seriously . . .

30

BERNARD: What about . . .?
ALAN: Can you come and see me tomorrow? At the house. We'll
    talk about things then.
BERNARD: Tomorrow?
ALAN: Yes, come and we'll talk tomorrow.

EXTERIOR. A FIELD. LATER THE SAME DAY
BERNARD *standing in the boat. Motionless. A state of shock.*

EXTERIOR. A FIELD. THE SAME DAY
We see the church in the distance from BERNARD's *point of view in the
boat.*

INTERIOR. THE CHURCH. LATER THE SAME DAY
*A shot of Bernard's boots. He has left them neatly inside the front door
of the church.* BERNARD *is lying on the floor of the aisle. Completely
spread-eagled. He is alone.*

EXTERIOR. OUTSIDE RAIF'S SIGNALBOX. THE SAME DAY
RAIF *is alone, sitting slumped over.* DOUGLAS *suddenly appears. He
doesn't notice, at first, that* RAIF *is in considerable distress.* RAIF *does
not see him, until he speaks.*
DOUGLAS: Raif? (*Intimately*) Are you all right? You look so unhappy.
RAIF: What?
    (*Pause.*)
DOUGLAS: Sorry if I . . . You know . .
RAIF: What?
DOUGLAS: What I mean is . . . I'm pleased . . .
RAIF: Pleased?
DOUGLAS: Pleased that you're not seeing her. It's the right thing.
    But I understand how difficult these things are.
RAIF: You do?
DOUGLAS: Of course I do.
    (DOUGLAS *is suddenly very awkward.*)
    Come and see me sometime . . . Will you?
RAIF: Right you are.
DOUGLAS: Good.
    (DOUGLAS *leaves.*)

INTERIOR. THE CHURCH. LATER THE SAME DAY
DOUGLAS *enters the church. He sees Bernard's boots. He sees*
BERNARD – *still lying on the floor, motionless.* DOUGLAS *approaches*
BERNARD *very cautiously. When he is very close he speaks – he leans*
over him.
DOUGLAS: Bernard Cross? Bernard Cross, isn't it?
    (BERNARD *looks up at him – but remains on the floor.*)
BERNARD: I don't want to go home . . .
DOUGLAS: Stay here.
BERNARD: Thank you, sir.
DOUGLAS: Do you need to talk to someone?
BERNARD: Don't need nothing.
    (*He stands up and starts to leave.*)
DOUGLAS: Can I help you?
BERNARD: Excuse me, sir. I'll be on my way now. Thank you for
    your trouble.
DOUGLAS: Nothing is any trouble.
BERNARD: I won't be stopping any longer. Thank you.
DOUGLAS: Bernard?
BERNARD: Yes, sir.
DOUGLAS: Come back here soon.
BERNARD: Come back?
DOUGLAS: Yes, you must come back soon . . .

EXTERIOR. OUTSIDE BERNARD'S HOUSE. DUSK
BERNARD *standing outside his house. The sound of rock music and*
voices from within. He goes up close to an open window and listens.

INTERIOR. THE KITCHEN. MOMENTS LATER
MAUD *gives* AMY *her supper.* AMY *starts eating.* JEN *is listening to a*
ghetto-blaster – sitting separately. Loud rock music.
MAUD: (*Angry*) Turn that thing down. I can't think.
    (BERNARD *comes into the kitchen.* MAUD *sees him.*)
    And where do you think you been? Hope you're not hungry,
    'cause dinner's ruined . . .
    (BERNARD *just stands there – expressionless.*)
    You could at least come home first before going off . . .
    Bernard . . .! Bernard?

32

(BERNARD *says nothing. He slowly walks towards Jen's ghetto-blaster. He picks it up and clumsily tries to turn it off.*)

JEN: I'm listening to that.

MAUD: Bernard? What's the matter, Bernard? What is it?

    (BERNARD *turns the music off. Silence.*)

BERNARD: (*To* MAUD) Been laid off, ain't I?

MAUD: You what?

BERNARD: Been laid off.

INTERIOR. ALAN BRANDON'S SITTING ROOM. NIGHT

ALAN *is alone. He is wearing pyjamas and a dressing gown. He is listening to a Beethoven string quartet. He hears several loud knocks.*

EXTERIOR. OUTSIDE ALAN BRANDON'S FRONT DOOR. NIGHT

MAUD *is banging on the front door.* AMY, *with one of Maud's scarves around her head to hide her new haircut, is standing next to her. She is crying.*

AMY: I want to go home now.

MAUD: *Please*, Amy.

    (ALAN BRANDON *eventually opens the door. Overlapping dialogue.*)

    You can't do this to us, Mr Brandon.

ALAN: Ah, Mrs Cross, I was expecting Bernard . . . Tomorrow.

MAUD: Well you got me . . . *Now*.

INTERIOR. ALAN BRANDON'S SITTING ROOM. THE SAME NIGHT

MAUD *and* AMY *are sitting together on a large sofa. As* MAUD *and* ALAN *talk, the camera favours* AMY. ALAN *stands while he speaks. A shot of Amy and Maud's muddy Wellington boots on Alan's carpet.*

ALAN: You must understand, Mrs Cross – Bernard's redundancy is not a personal issue. It's an unfortunate commercial necessity. No other reason.

MAUD: (*Interrupting*) It's not right to take away a man's job when he's worked for you all his life . . . Good work too . . . I got a family to feed . . . And you talk to me about reason . . . (*Pause.*)

ALAN: Mrs Cross?

MAUD: What?

(ALAN *walks around the room evasively – he momentarily touches a photograph of his dead wife.*)

ALAN: I was wondering whether you would feel able to come and help me out with the cleaning, here in the house – on a regular basis, of course . . . Is that something you might feel able to do? Think about it, anyway . . . It would certainly be a great help to me.

INTERIOR. BERNARD'S HOUSE. THE KITCHEN. THE SAME NIGHT

BERNARD, MAUD, AMY *and* JEN.

BERNARD: (*Violently*) You done what? You'd clean up after Alan Brandon? (*Slight pause.*) Have you no pride?

MAUD: We need the money . . .

INTERIOR. A TRAIN. DAY

BRIAN, *a commuter, is returning from work. He takes a photograph of Bernard's house as he passes. He looks pleased with himself. He uses a very sophisticated camera.*

INTERIOR/EXTERIOR. MAUD'S KITCHEN/THE CORRIDOR. DAY

BERNARD *is doing nothing, except look out of the window. We hear the train passing in the distance.* JEN *is applying eye makeup and fingernail varnish.* BERNARD *turns to look at* JEN, *who is sitting at the table. Pause.*

JEN: What you staring for?

BERNARD: Nothing . . . Can look at you, can't I?

JEN: What for?

BERNARD: Nothing . . . You look real nice. (*Pause.*) Going to see your boyfriend, are you? (*Slight pause.*) Have you got a boyfriend?

JEN: Shut up . . . And stop staring, I don't like it, right?

BERNARD: No need to be like that . . . No need at all. (*Self-pitying*) You should be nice to me.

JEN: *Stop* staring.

(*The sound of an F111 passing overhead.*)

34

EXTERIOR. THE FENS. THE SAME DAY
An F111 flies overhead, describing a wide arc across the sky.

INTERIOR. THE KITCHEN IN ALAN BRANDON'S HOUSE. THE
SAME DAY
*The sound of the F111. ALAN is sitting at the table doing paperwork.
It is a large, traditional-looking kitchen. Oak furniture and an Aga.
MAUD is scrubbing the brick floor in the hallway. ALAN can see her
through the open door. He watches her – sexual tension. AMY follows
MAUD as she cleans, like a shadow.*
ALAN: Hello Amy . . . You don't say very much, do you?
MAUD: You're shy, aren't you Amy?
AMY: (*Quietly*) No.
ALAN: (*To* MAUD) How's your eldest? What's her name?
    Jennifer?
MAUD: Jen? Oh, she's fine . . .
ALAN: Lovely girl.
MAUD: Thank you very much.
    (*Pause.*)
ALAN: And, what about *you*?
MAUD: Sorry?
ALAN: Everything all right?
MAUD: Not use to bricks – we got lino.
ALAN: They look fine to me. It's been a long time since they
    looked like that.
MAUD: I'll get 'em looking all right.
    (MAUD *is now cleaning underneath Alan's chair.* ALAN *is
    enjoying watching her.*)
ALAN: Weather's looking up.
MAUD: I don't like it when it's hot . . . So, who else you laid off?
ALAN: Bernard is the first. But there will have to be others . . .
    Well, I shall have to be getting along. Thank you for your
    help. Your money's in an envelope in the hall. I'll see you
    tomorrow . . .
MAUD: Right you are.
ALAN: Goodbye, Amy.
MAUD: (*To* AMY) Say goodbye, Amy.
AMY: (*Quietly*) No.

(ALAN *laughs, then leaves – tip-toeing across the wet floor.*)

INTERIOR. MAUD'S KITCHEN. DAY

MAUD *is scrubbing the floor, on her hands and knees.* BERNARD *sitting doing nothing.*

MAUD: It's been two weeks now – and what have you done? Well, what have you done? Bernard?

BERNARD: What?

MAUD: I said what have you done?

BERNARD: Nothing. I i'n't done nothing. (*Pause.*) So what do *you* do?

MAUD: What?

BERNARD: So what do you do in the house of Alan Brandon's?

MAUD: What d'you think I do? Move your feet.

BERNARD: If I knew I wouldn't be asking, would I?

MAUD: Well, use your head . . . I do the same as I do here. Bernard, move yourself, will you?

BERNARD: It's my bloody house, you know.

MAUD: It's not your house – it's Alan Brandon's house, and lucky for us, Alan Brandon's letting us stop . . .

BERNARD: Shut up, woman.

MAUD: Don't talk like that. I'm trying to clean up . . . Two houses i'n't easy, you know.

(BERNARD *picks up the rubbish bin and begins to empty it on to the floor.*)

BERNARD: Clean that up then. And that.

MAUD: Clean that up. This instant, Bernard.

(BERNARD *continues to tip the rubbish. Overlapping dialogue.*)

BERNARD: Shut your face.

MAUD: Clean it up. Who d'you think you are?

BERNARD: You bloody clean it up. You clean it up. You can clean up my rubbish as well as Alan Brandon's.

MAUD: Clean it up, Bernard.

BERNARD: Give me money. Give me ten pound. Give it me.

(BERNARD *grabs* MAUD'S *purse, which is in the pocket of her apron. She tries to stop him.*)

MAUD: (*Resisting*) What you doing? What you doing? I haven't any money to give you. I haven't enough . . .

BERNARD: Plenty more you can get like that. Plenty more where

that come from.
(BERNARD *leaves, slamming the door.* MAUD *looks at the rubbish on the floor.*)

EXTERIOR. THE SIGNALBOX. DAY
JEN, AMY *and* RAIF. JEN *and* AMY *are outside.*
JEN: Come to see you.
RAIF: What for?
AMY: Because.

INTERIOR. A BARN. THE SAME DAY
JEN, RAIF *and* AMY. AMY *sits between them.*
RAIF: Me old girl i'n't well.
AMY: Why?
RAIF: She's so old . . . Keeps sleeping . . .
AMY: Well, my Dad's got laid off.
JEN: Shut up, Amy.
RAIF: Has he? Jen?
JEN: What?
RAIF: Has he been laid off?
JEN: I don't care, Raif. That's not why I come here.
   (*Pause.*)
RAIF: (*To* JEN) What you bring her for?
AMY: She has to.
JEN: Don't.
   (*Pause.*)
RAIF: Can't *do* nothing then.
JEN: Can.
RAIF: Can't do nothing with her here, I mean.
JEN: Can so.
RAIF: Come here, then.
   (JEN *moves across to* RAIF. *Camera holds on* AMY'*s face.*)
AMY: (*Loudly*) I'm going.
JEN: (*Voice-over*) Go, then.

EXTERIOR/INTERIOR. THE BARN. DAY
A wide shot of the barn. AMY *leaves. She hesitates, then goes back to spy on* RAIF *and* JEN. *We see them making love from* AMY'*s point of view.*

INTERIOR. THE BARN. LATER THE SAME DAY
Time has passed.
RAIF: I saw your Dad going in the church.
JEN: I don't want to talk about me Dad.
RAIF: Why?
JEN: Just don't.

INTERIOR. JOAN BENSON'S SHOP. LATER THE SAME DAY
JOAN *is asleep.* AMY *enters. The bell rings but does not wake* JOAN.
*She is sitting in an old comfortable chair by the counter. Her head is on
one side. She is breathing heavily.* AMY *looks at her. She steals several
bars of chocolate and packets of sweets. She leaves the shop. The bell
rings again as she goes out.* JOAN *doesn't stir.*

EXTERIOR. THE FENS. NIGHT
A train passes in the night.

EXTERIOR. THE FENS. DAY
*An 'American'-looking landscape – crooked telegraph poles stretch into
the distance.*

INTERIOR. JEN AND AMY'S BEDROOM. DAY
JEN *applies lipstick at her dressing table, in front of the large
American flag.*

INTERIOR. MAUD'S KITCHEN. DAY
AMY *listens to* MAUD *and* BERNARD *talking, from behind the kitchen
door. The first part of the scene is played on* AMY.
MAUD: (*Voice-over*) Did you look in the paper? There are jobs, if
    you look . . . This can't go on . . .
    (MAUD *looks out of the window.*)
BERNARD: Come here love . . . (*Pause.*) Come here . . .
MAUD: What you want?
BERNARD: Come here.
MAUD: What is it, Bernard? What you want?
BERNARD: Remember when we were courting? Remember where
    we did it? Do you remember, love? We did it in the living

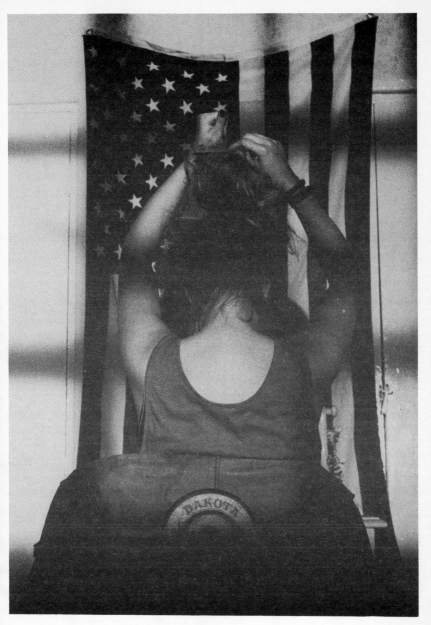

room at your Mum and Dad's . . . By the fire . . . Nowhere
else to do it were there? It were nice, weren't it? You liked it,
didn't you?

MAUD: You know I did . . . Wouldn't have done it otherwise,
would I? It were nice . . . What's got into you Bernard?

BERNARD: They could have come in any time . . . Just walked
right in. Never did mind, and seen us there doing it on the
carpet with the bits of coal that got every place you didn't
want 'em.

(BERNARD *laughs*. MAUD *laughs*.)

MAUD: What's made you think of that, Bernard?

BERNARD: I liked it, you liked it. You with your arse in the air.

MAUD: Course I liked it, Bernard. What you thinking of? What's
got into you?

BERNARD: I want it now.

MAUD: Don't be soft, Bernard . . .

BERNARD: I want it right now . . . Right here, like then.

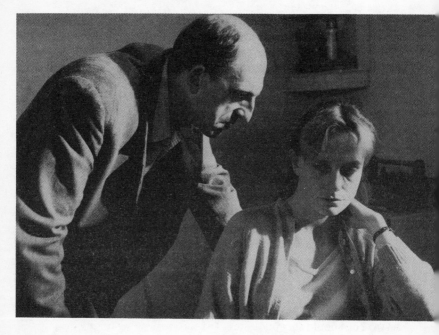

MAUD: Amy's still . . .

BERNARD: (*Interrupting*) Come here, I want to smell you.

MAUD: Amy will hear . . .

BERNARD: I want to smell you.

MAUD: What are you, soft in the head?

BERNARD: Come here, that's real exciting that is, with Amy
   coming in any time . . . Come here . . .

MAUD: Don't be so damned soft, Bernard.

   (*Cut to* AMY.)

BERNARD: (*Sudden aggression*) Come here . . .

   (*Pause.* MAUD *flinches with fear.* AMY *runs away, as* BERNARD
   opens the door to leave.)

EXTERIOR. THE FOOTBRIDGE NEAR THE SIGNALBOX. DAY
BERNARD, *on his way to the church, crosses the footbridge.*

EXTERIOR. UNDER THE FOOTBRIDGE. A MOMENT LATER
RAIF *and* JEN *are sitting beneath the bridge. They hear* BERNARD.

RAIF: He's going to the church again.

   (JEN *looks away. She gives the impression of not being
   interested.*)

EXTERIOR. A GRAVEYARD. THE SAME DAY
*The graveyard behind Douglas Stonea's church. It is very run down.
The gravestones are all at oblique angles on account of the soft peat
soil. The graveyard is overhung with yew trees. The grass between the
gravestones is very green and mossy.* BERNARD *is standing alone
amongst the gravestones.*

EXTERIOR. UNDER THE FOOTBRIDGE. THE SAME DAY
JEN *and* RAIF.

JEN: I want something to 'appen . . . I want to go away.

RAIF: Where?

JEN: Away from here. Away from you.

RAIF: You shouldn't want to go away. How d'you know away i'n't
   as boring as here?

JEN: Don't be daft.

RAIF: You should stay put, like I do . . . 'Cause we belong. Not

41

like others – them what comes here and don't belong.

JEN: Don't try and be clever.

RAIF: Don't care what you say . . . I'm staying put. So should you. (*Pause.*) Do you want to do it?

JEN: Not with you.

RAIF: What's that meant to mean?

JEN: Nothing . . . I'm going.

RAIF: Where?

JEN: Don't know.

　　　(*Overlapping dialogue.*)

RAIF: Don't go, Jen.

JEN: I'll do what I like, Raif.

RAIF: Don't go.

JEN: Try and stop me.

RAIF: I will.

　　　(JEN *starts to go.* RAIF *grabs her.*)

JEN: Get off me. Fuck off.

RAIF: (*Desperate*) Jen!

(*He holds her hard. She kicks him. After a violent struggle,* RAIF
lets her break free. RAIF *is left slumped on the ground.*)

EXTERIOR. THE FENS. LATER THE SAME DAY
JEN *walks alone. She looks up at an* F*III*.

INTERIOR. JEN AND AMY'S BEDROOM. NIGHT
JEN *lies in bed, unable to sleep.*

EXTERIOR. BERNARD'S HOUSE. NIGHT
The house is in darkness, apart from the light from Jen's room.

EXTERIOR. OUTSIDE BERNARD'S HOUSE. DAY
BERNARD *is hiding outside the house. He watches* AMY *and* MAUD
leave. He stands up and walks towards the house.

INTERIOR. ALAN BRANDON'S BEDROOM. DAY
MAUD *is putting Alan's clothes away.* ALAN *enters.*
ALAN: Mrs Cross, can I have a word?
MAUD: If you like.
ALAN: Come and sit down.
      (*He indicates the end of the bed.*)
MAUD: If you like.
      (*An awkward pause.*)
ALAN: This *is* difficult.
      (*Pause. He seems to be about to make a sexual advance.*)
      Mrs Cross?
MAUD: Mr Brandon?
ALAN: Now, the other day I noticed that some money went
      missing from the sideboard . . .
MAUD: I put it back . . . I did. Next day . . . After you paid
      me . . . Swear I did. Needed it quick though.
ALAN: I know you put it back. It just seemed strange to me that
      you didn't feel able to ask me for an advance.
MAUD: (*Very upset*) Didn't know how to say that . . .
      (*Pause.* ALAN *sits next to her.*)
ALAN: (*Intimately*) You're an honest woman, I know that. You're
      a good woman. So, next time all you have to do is ask . . .

43

You're already a great help to me, Mrs Cross.

MAUD: That's good . . .

ALAN: I'm beginning to wonder how I ever managed without you . . .
So next time all you have to do is ask. I'm a fair man, Mrs Cross.
(ALAN *puts his arm behind* MAUD – *without touching her*.)

MAUD: (*Standing*) Won't happen again. Thank you very much.
And now I must be getting on.
(MAUD *returns to her work*. ALAN *leaves the room*.)

INTERIOR. MAUD'S KITCHEN. DAY
BERNARD *sitting at the table*. JEN *sitting on the other side*. BERNARD *is doing nothing*. JEN *is sewing a US Airforce badge on to her jacket*.

44

BERNARD: Jen?

JEN: What?

BERNARD: What time is your Mum and Amy getting in?

JEN: How should I know?

(*Pause.*)

BERNARD: I've been thinking about you today . . . What d'you want to do? (*Slight pause.*) What d'you want to be?

JEN: How should I know. Not getting married.

BERNARD: Why?

JEN: Shut up.

(*Pause.*)

(*Reluctantly, half to herself*) Hairdresser.

BERNARD: What?

JEN: (*Aggressively*) Hairdresser. Soon as I can, I'm going away. Get away from you.

BERNARD: Didn't know that. Didn't know you wanted to be a hairdresser.

JEN: Course you didn't.

BERNARD: What you want to go away for?

JEN: Others don't, but I do. Shut up will you?

(*Pause.*)

BERNARD: Do mine if you want . . .

JEN: What?

BERNARD: Do my hair if you want.

JEN: Don't be daft.

BERNARD: Well you can if you want.

JEN: Don't be daft. Look at it.

BERNARD: What d'you mean? If you want to be a hairdresser, you could start with mine. Practice. Could do with a trim.

JEN: You 'aven't got any. Shut up will you. (*Pause.*) Just smell your feet.

BERNARD: What d'you mean?

JEN: Put your shoes on, will you?

BERNARD: Don't smell.

JEN: Do. It's disgusting.

(BERNARD *tries to smell his feet.*)

Can't you wash 'em or nothing?

(BERNARD *takes off his socks. He starts washing his feet in a*

bucket.)
Not in there. That's for the floor.
(BERNARD *continues to wash his feet. Pause. Having done so, he moves over next to* JEN. *He is barefoot*.)

BERNARD: That's better, eh?
(BERNARD *puts his arm around* JEN.)

JEN: Get off.
(BERNARD *tries to touch her head.* JEN *moves away.* BERNARD *reaches out again. He tries to embrace her. It turns into a struggle.* JEN *breaks free. She is terrified of him*.)
Get off me. Leave me be. Fuck off . . .

BERNARD: I'm going out.

JEN: Good.
(BERNARD *picks up his shoes*.)

BERNARD: I'm going out then.
(BERNARD *starts to leave*.)

JEN: Good.
(BERNARD *leaves, still barefoot, carrying his shoes. We hear him leave the house.* JEN *is pleased to be alone*.)

EXTERIOR. RAIF'S SIGNALBOX. THE SAME DAY
RAIF *sees* BERNARD *walking towards the church.* RAIF *checks the timetable and looks at the clock*.

EXTERIOR. NEAR THE CHURCH. A MOMENT LATER
RAIF *follows* BERNARD, *who is walking through the graveyard*.

EXTERIOR. GRAVEYARD. A MOMENT LATER
From RAIF's *point of view, we see* BERNARD, *who is standing beside a bench which has been built around a tree.* DOUGLAS *appears.* RAIF *keeps himself out of sight, but creeps closer to overhear their conversation*.

DOUGLAS: Bernard! You came back.

BERNARD: Well, you said to come back.

DOUGLAS: (*Sitting*) How are things?
(BERNARD *sits. Pause*.)

BERNARD: What things?

DOUGLAS: How's the family?

46

BERNARD: Family?
DOUGLAS: Everything all right?
BERNARD: Nothing's all right.
DOUGLAS: I see. (*Slight pause.*) How's Jennifer?
BERNARD: Jen?
DOUGLAS: Yes, how's Jen?
BERNARD: What about her?
DOUGLAS: I know *all* about Jennifer.
BERNARD: You do?
DOUGLAS: Indeed I do.
　　(*Pause.*)
BERNARD: You know all about what's happened?
DOUGLAS: Yes.
BERNARD: I'm not a good man, Mr Stonea.

47

DOUGLAS: I'm sorry?

(*Pause.*)

BERNARD: (*Speaking slowly*) When I'm buried, I don't want no
'eadstone over my 'ead. Not at all . . . Is it wrong to? . . . If
you have nothing . . . Is it wrong? Is it wrong? I'm not a good
man, Mr Stonea, that's the truth . . . It's only folks who die
young should have an 'eadstone . . . When I'm buried I don't
want no 'eadstone, right . . . Will you see to it? The love you
leave behind should be your memorial – not 'eadstone – I've
used up all my love now . . . What you got, Mr Stonea, if
you've used up all the love you were give? Tell me that . . .

(*Pause.* DOUGLAS *and* BERNARD *look at each other.*)

DOUGLAS: We're alike, you know . . . You and I.

BERNARD: I don't want no memorial . . . Will you see to it, Mr
Stonea?

(BERNARD *stands.*)

I must be going now, if you'll excuse me.

DOUGLAS: Come back soon, Bernard.

(BERNARD *walks away.* RAIF *hides as he passes him.*)

INTERIOR. RAIF'S SIGNALBOX. LATER THE SAME DAY
Close-up of the clock. The train is due in five minutes.

EXTERIOR. THE GRAVEYARD. THE SAME DAY
DOUGLAS *is still sitting on his own.* RAIF *is still hiding behind a
headstone. He looks at his watch. He moves, making a noise.*
DOUGLAS *looks up.* RAIF *is very still, not daring to make a sound.*
DOUGLAS *stands up and goes into the church.* RAIF *leaves.*

EXTERIOR. THE RAILWAY BRIDGE OVER THE RIVER. LATER
THE SAME DAY
BERNARD *is alone. He walks towards the railway bridge along the
river bank. Under the bridge is a length of rope. He picks it up and
climbs on to the bridge.*

EXTERIOR. THE SIGNALBOX. DAY
RAIF *opens the gates and the train passes through.*

EXTERIOR. THE RAILWAY BRIDGE. THE SAME DAY
BERNARD *ties one end of the rope around the rails and stretches the rest of the rope to the other side of the bridge. He ties a length of iron to one of his ankles and puts a weight around his neck. He ties a noose in the rope and puts his neck through it. He puts his ear to the rails.*

EXTERIOR. THE RAILWAY BRIDGE. DAY
The train approaches the bridge.

EXTERIOR. THE RAILWAY BRIDGE. DAY
BERNARD *jumps over the side of the bridge – hanging himself. His feet are almost touching the surface of the water.*

EXTERIOR. THE RAILWAY BRIDGE. THE SAME DAY
BERNARD's *hanging body is seen in silhouette. The train approaches. As it passes over the bridge it cuts through the rope.* BERNARD's *body and the rope drop into the water, leaving no trace.*

INTERIOR. THE COCKPIT OF AN FIII. DAY
JACOB *spins through 360 degrees: the world turned upside-down.*

EXTERIOR. THE FENS. DAY
The search for BERNARD. *Volunteers and police appear from two converging rows of trees.*

INTERIOR. MAUD'S KITCHEN. DAY
MAUD, AMY *and* JEN *together.* JEN *and* AMY *sit at the table.* MAUD *stands separately, her back to us, looking out of the window.* JEN *is wearing no makeup.* AMY *and* JEN *talk in whispers, unheard by* MAUD.
AMY: Jen?
JEN: Mmm?
AMY: Where's he gone?
JEN: Away.
AMY: What if he don't ever come back?
JEN: You should be glad.
AMY: Why?
JEN: Because.

INTERIOR. THE CHURCH VESTRY. DAY
DOUGLAS *is alone.*

EXTERIOR. THE GRAVEYARD. DAY
The graveyard is empty. A train passes across the horizon.

INTERIOR. JOAN'S BEDROOM. NIGHT
JOAN *prays beside her bed.*

INTERIOR. ALAN BRANDON'S HOUSE. THE STAIRCASE. DAY
MAUD *is scrubbing the stairway carpet.* ALAN *appears, his face peering through the bannisters from below.*
ALAN: Strange business.
MAUD: Sorry, Mr Brandon?
ALAN: I said, 'Strange business' . . . It must be a great shock for you, Mrs Cross. It's a shock for all of us, of course. A man doesn't just disappear for no reason. One feels so responsible – doesn't one?
MAUD: You what?
ALAN: Doesn't matter. (*Pause.*) So how do you feel?
MAUD: I'd rather not, Mr Brandon – if you don't mind – I'd rather not.
ALAN: I'm sorry – I didn't mean to . . .
   (*He leaves.* MAUD *continues with her work.*)

EXTERIOR. THE FENS. DAY
Bright sunlight. JEN *and* AMY *are walking slowly along the river bank.* JEN *is ahead,* AMY *lagging some way behind – almost as if they are attached to each other by an invisible cord.*
AMY: (*Calling after* JEN) We'll find him.
JEN: Come on.
AMY: I'm too tired.
   (*They both stop walking, at exactly the same moment.* JEN *turns around to face* AMY.)
JEN: Go home then.
   (JEN *turns her back on* AMY *and continues alone.* AMY *stands still for a moment and watches her go – then she turns back.*)

EXTERIOR. THE FENS. THE SAME DAY
JEN *continues alone.*

EXTERIOR. A CLEARING BY THE RIVER BANK. THE SAME
DAY
*A quiet and mysterious place bordered on one side by the river dyke and
on the other by a vast expanse of fields. Overhung with trees on all
sides – the place has obviously been used for many years as an
unofficial dump for old farm machinery. There are old pieces of farm
equipment lying disused and covered by grass. The trees have a slightly
strange aspect; many have Dutch Elm disease and their bare branches
stand out like gnarled fingers against the sky. Also dumped here is an
old Mercedes, its grey paintwork peeling. It is tilted on one side into the
ground. Around it many wild flowers. The sound of blues guitar. The
camera moves closer to the car to reveal* JACOB, *lost in thought.*

EXTERIOR. THE CLEARING. A MOMENT LATER
JEN *is looking at* JACOB. JACOB *has not yet seen her. The music
continues. She slowly and quietly approaches him. Her face is running
with tears. After a while he looks up. He doesn't register any surprise
at seeing her. With tears still running down her face, she is now very
close – she reaches out and touches him – as if to find out if he is real.
She looks frightened. He draws her close. They kiss.*

EXTERIOR. OUTSIDE RAIF'S SIGNALBOX. LATER THE SAME
DAY
AMY *is walking home on her own.* RAIF *sees her. He calls out.*
RAIF:Amy! Amy!
    (AMY *pretends not to hear.*)
    Amy!
AMY: What?
RAIF: Where's Jen?
AMY: Don't know. (*Pause.*) She don't want you no more. (*Pause.*)
RAIF: Why don't she?
AMY: Got to go home now.
    (*She walks away.* RAIF *turns back.*)

51

INTERIOR. THE MERCEDES. LATER THE SAME DAY
JACOB *and* JEN *make love.*

EXTERIOR. THE RAILWAY CROSSING. THE SAME DAY
RAIF *watches a train pass through.*

INTERIOR. JOAN'S BEDROOM. LATE AT NIGHT
RAIF *is sitting by* JOAN's *bedside.* JOAN *is lying with her eyes closed.*
Long silence.
JOAN: (*Quietly*) Now, your mother said – you weren't meant. But
    I said, 'You got to look to 'em – whatever.' (*Pause.*) You got
    to look to others, not just your own. (*Pause.*) Right?
RAIF: Right.

EXTERIOR. DAKOTA ROAD. DAY
JEN, *alone, staring through the security fence. She watches an* F III
preparing to take off.

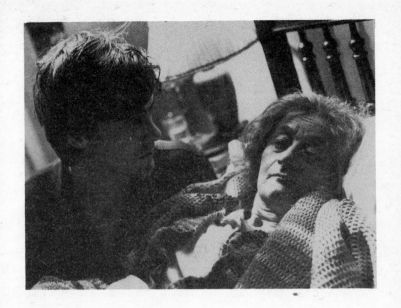

INTERIOR. THE CHURCH. DAY
Joan's flowers are dead.

INTERIOR. JOAN'S BEDROOM. NIGHT
RAIF *is putting* JOAN *to bed.*

INTERIOR. JOAN'S SITTING ROOM. DAY
Morning sunlight fills the room. JOAN *is laid out in the front room.*
Only her face is visible. DOUGLAS *and* RAIF *sit beside the body.*
DOUGLAS: Did she ask for me?
    (RAIF *shakes his head. They both sit in silence for a while.*)
    So what are you going to do?
RAIF: Nothing.
DOUGLAS: (*Intimately*) I'd like to help you in any way I can.
RAIF: Don't want your help.
DOUGLAS: I see.
    (*Pause.* RAIF *looks at* JOAN.)
RAIF: Her God weren't your God – that I do know. *Her* God were

a God of love . . . A God of light . . . I ain't got no God. Don't
want one neither.
(*Pause.*)
DOUGLAS: A God of light?
RAIF: What you doing here, anyhow? I don't want you here.
Right?

INTERIOR. JOAN'S BEDROOM. THE SAME DAY
RAIF *is using the dressing-table mirror in Joan's bedroom to get
changed for the funeral service. He is wearing an uncomfortable and
ill-fitting grey suit. He is struggling with a tie. His face and eyes are
swollen. On the dresser, a delicate framed embroidery,* 'IN GOD WE
TRUST'.

INTERIOR. ALAN BRANDON'S STUDY. DAY
MAUD *is cleaning the window next to the telescope.* AMY *is with her.*
ALAN *comes in. He looks very pleased. He is carrying a plaque in
Joan's memory. The sound of a single church bell in the distance.*

ALAN: Well, what do you think, Mrs Cross?
   (*He shows her the plaque.*)
MAUD: Very nice.
ALAN: Douglas is going to have it placed beside the organ. My
   little contribution. She won't be forgotten.
MAUD: Didn't know her. Not really.
ALAN: (*Admiring the plaque*) It was quite a job to get it ready for
   the service this afternoon. If you have a moment, Mrs Cross
   – I need to have a word with you . . . alone.
MAUD: Oh yes?
ALAN: Yes, please. A business matter.

EXTERIOR. ALAN BRANDON'S HOUSE. A SHORT TIME LATER
AMY *leaves the house. The sound of the church bell – slightly louder.*

INTERIOR. ALAN BRANDON'S STUDY. THE SAME DAY. A FEW
MOMENTS LATER
MAUD *is sitting,* ALAN *standing and pacing about as he talks. He
continually returns to Joan's plaque, which is propped up on his desk,
admiring it as he speaks.*
ALAN: I shall come straight to the point – it concerns the tied
   cottage. I am going to have to sell it.
MAUD: I don't believe it . . .
ALAN: It's true.
MAUD: That's my home . . .
ALAN: (*Interrupting*) Not strictly, Mrs Cross . . . I have, however –
   as I feel some obligation to you and your daughters – found
   an alternative arrangement. You understand this is not a
   legal obligation but it is something I feel *morally* inclined to
   provide.
MAUD: What alternative?
ALAN: A caravan.
MAUD: A what?
ALAN: Well, a trailer-home, actually, Mrs Cross, with
   amenities . . . An offer I could not refuse. I'd like you to
   meet him, obviously. Seemed a very nice man to me. You see
   he's always fancied the house. Used to admire it on the train,
   he said.

MAUD: Meet him?

ALAN: (*Laughing*) Yes, and you never know, he might need a
cleaner. I'll recommend you . . . Only joking. Life goes on,
Mrs Cross – I won't let you down. Now, I must hurry, or I'll
miss the service.

EXTERIOR. THE CHURCH. THE SAME DAY
AMY *is hiding behind a tree with a view of the front porch of the
church. Many people are walking towards the church.* DOUGLAS
welcomes them. The sound of the bell. ALAN *arrives, in a hurry.*
DOUGLAS *welcomes him warmly and admires the plaque which* ALAN
shows him.

EXTERIOR. A ROAD. SOME TIME LATER
JEN *walking towards the church. The sound of the congregation
singing.*

INTERIOR. THE CHURCH. DAY
*The service has begun. The congregation is singing the Charles Wesley
hymn that* JOAN *sang at the beginning of the film. The church is almost
full. The singing is rich and fills the church.* RAIF *is positioned in the
front row, to the left of the coffin. He is alone and looks isolated.* ALAN
*is singing very loudly and is positioned on the right-hand side of the
altar.* DOUGLAS *looks feverish.*

EXTERIOR. THE CHURCH. A SHORT TIME LATER
JEN *sees* AMY. *The singing carries easily across to them.*

JEN: Amy.

AMY: Where you been?

JEN: Away . . . What you doing?

AMY: Watching.
(*They stand together, closely, intimately.* JEN *leaves* AMY *and
walks towards the front door of the church.*)

INTERIOR. THE CHURCH. A SHORT TIME LATER
The end of the hymn. We see the congregation from DOUGLAS's *point
of view.*

DOUGLAS: Please be seated.

(*The congregation sit, except for* RAIF. DOUGLAS *looks at him.*)
Please be seated.
(*Pause.* RAIF *slowly sits.* DOUGLAS *clears his throat.*)
Jesus said, I am the resurrection, and I am the life; he who
believes in me, though he die, yet shall he live, and he who
lives and believes in me shall never die.
(RAIF'*s face looks puzzled, questioning.* DOUGLAS *clears his
throat.*)
We believe that Jesus died and rose again . . .
(DOUGLAS *sees* JEN *enter surreptitiously at the back of the
church.*)
. . . and so it will be for those who die as Christians.
(RAIF *looks around and sees* JEN. *He stands.*)
God will bring them to life with Jesus.
RAIF: What?
DOUGLAS: (*Quietly*) Please sit down, Raif.
RAIF:(*Raises his voice*) What you on about? She i'n't coming back
. . . What you on about?
(RAIF *leaves his pew and starts down the aisle.* JEN *disappears
through the partly open door. There is a stunned silence as* RAIF
leaves. DOUGLAS *tries to continue.* ALAN *looks outraged by*
RAIF'*s behaviour.*
DOUGLAS: Thus we shall always be with the Lord. Comfort one
another with these words.
(RAIF *returns to face* DOUGLAS.)
RAIF: (*Shouting*) Bernard Cross, he i'n't coming back, neither . . .
and you damned well know it . . .
(*He turns and runs out of the church.*)

EXTERIOR. THE CHURCH. A MOMENT LATER
RAIF *runs out of the church.* JEN *has gone.* AMY *is still standing there.*
RAIF: (To AMY)
Where is she?
AMY: That way.
(*She points in the direction* JEN *went.*)

EXTERIOR. THE FENS. A MOMENT LATER
RAIF *looking for* JEN.

EXTERIOR. THE FENS. A FEW MOMENTS LATER
RAIF *alone.* JEN *is nowhere to be seen.*
RAIF: Jen!
    (*Pause. He looks around. Complete silence.*)
    I told 'em all what's what, Jen. (*Quieter*) Jen.
    (*Silence. He turns away.*)

EXTERIOR. THE FENS. A SHORT TIME LATER
JEN *approaches the mysterious place; she is out of breath. She looks at
the empty Mercedes.*

INTERIOR/EXTERIOR. JEN'S BEDROOM. DAY
JEN *is tearing down the American posters. She looks out of the
window. All the family's belongings are being moved out into a trailer
attached to the back of Alan's Range Rover.* ALAN *is helping* MAUD.

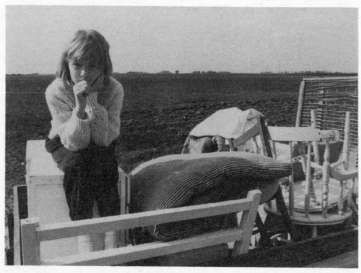

EXTERIOR. OUTSIDE BERNARD'S HOUSE. THE SAME DAY
ALAN *and* MAUD *continue to put furniture into the trailer.* JEN *comes
out of the house with her arms full of posters and pictures taken down
from the wall.* ALAN *sees her. He watches her. He goes over to her.*

ALAN: We'll have to make a big bonfire, eh Jen?
JEN: Do what you like.

EXTERIOR. OUTSIDE BERNARD'S HOUSE. DUSK
A big bonfire, tended by ALAN.

EXTERIOR. RAIF'S SIGNALBOX. DAY. TIME HAS PASSED
*Adjoining Raif's signalbox is a small platform; the trains only stop
here occasionally though.* RAIF *is opening the gates to the crossing.*

EXTERIOR. RAIF'S SIGNALBOX. THE SAME DAY
A train draws into the station. BRIAN *gets out.* RAIF *watches him
pass.* BRIAN *waves with a friendly smile.* RAIF *does not react.*

EXTERIOR. A TRACK NEAR MAUD'S OLD HOUSE. DAY
MAUD *is walking with* AMY. MAUD *looks towards her old house,
standing out in the distance. She sees* BRIAN *walk along the small
unlevelled road and into the house.*

EXTERIOR. BEHIND ALAN'S HOUSE. DAY. LATE SUMMER
The caravan is situated behind Alan's house. MAUD *is sitting alone at
the door of the caravan.* AMY *is separate, sitting on the ground,
burning insects with a magnifying glass.*

INTERIOR. THE CARAVAN. LATE AT NIGHT
AMY *is asleep.* JEN *and* MAUD *whisper so as not to wake* AMY.
JEN: Mum?
MAUD: What?
JEN: Where's Dad?
MAUD: Don't know.
JEN: Do you care, though?
MAUD: Course I do.
      (*Slight pause.*)
JEN: Is he dead?
MAUD: Don't know . . . But he's gone . . .
      It's probably for the best . . . (*Pause.*)
JEN: Mum?
MAUD: What? (*Pause.*)

JEN: I'm pregnant.
MAUD: You what?
JEN: I'm pregnant.
MAUD: You're not.
JEN: It's true.
MAUD: Whose is it?
AMY: What?
MAUD: Who's the father?
JEN: Don't know.
MAUD: What d'you mean, you don't know?
JEN: Not for sure, anyroad.
    (*Pause.*)
MAUD: You can't have it.
JEN: I can.
MAUD: You can't stay here, then.
JEN: I know.

EXTERIOR. THE CARAVAN. DAY

A shot of ALAN *passing a window in the house, which overlooks the caravan.* AMY *is sitting on the steps of the caravan,* MAUD *standing beside her.*

MAUD: Jen's leaving.

AMY: Why?

MAUD: 'Cause I said she 'ad to.

AMY: What for?

MAUD: 'Cause she's got to look to herself. (*Pause.*) Amy?

AMY: What?

MAUD: I'm not a good Mum. (*Slight pause.*) You like me, don't you?

AMY: Course I do.
MAUD: We'll get by, eh?
    (AMY *nods*.)
AMY: I'm going away one day . . . OK?
    (MAUD *nods*.)

EXTERIOR. THE CLEARING. AUTUMN DAY
The sun is shining. JEN *has returned to the place where she met*
JACOB. *The Mercedes is empty.* JEN *gets into the car. She examines*
her belly. There is no sign of JACOB's *presence. Suddenly the sound of*
someone. She looks up; RAIF *is standing nearby.*
RAIF: Followed you . . . What are you doing?
JEN: Nothing. (*Pause.*)
RAIF: You come here before?
JEN: No.
RAIF: Nice, i'n't it? (*Slight pause.*)
JEN: I'm not going away.
RAIF: Good. (*Slight pause.*)
JEN: Come 'ere, Raif.
    (RAIF *walks towards her.*)
    I'm not going away. Staying with you. All right?
RAIF: Right.

INTERIOR. THE SIGNALBOX. DAY
RAIF *and* JEN *together. They sit in silence. The stove is alight.* RAIF *is*
looking out across the fens.
RAIF: Jen? Got to tell you something I know.
JEN: What? (*Slight pause.*)
RAIF: I reckon I know more about your Dad . . . what happened
    . . . than I let on I did.
JEN: I don't care. I don't want to hear it.
RAIF: Why?
JEN: 'Cause that'll be your secret.
RAIF: Secret?
JEN: Yup. You keep it. 'Cause I don't want to know.
RAIF: Right.
JEN: Come here.
    (*She pulls him towards her. They embrace. Each looking over the*

63

other's shoulder, out across the fens in opposite directions. RAIF *is smiling,* JEN *has tears in her eyes. An* F111 *thunders overhead.* JEN *looks up momentarily and watches it disappear. She takes* RAIF's *face in her hands and looks at him. She starts to smile.* RAIF *stops smiling – tears come to his eyes.*)

RAIF: What is it? Jen?

JEN: Raif?

RAIF: What?

JEN: Nothing. Raif?

RAIF: What?

JEN: Nothing. (*Casually*) Love you.
　　(*A train passes through.*)

EXTERIOR. THE RAILWAY TRACK. A MOMENT LATER
The train disappearing into the distance.

EXTERIOR. A LONG STRAIGHT ROAD
AMY, *wearing a coat, walks away along a road which stretches for as far as the eye can see.*